CYBERSPIES

INSIDE THE WORLD OF
HACKING,
ONLINE PRIVACY,
AND CYBERTERRORISM

MICHAEL MILLER

TWENTY-FIRST CENTURY BOOKS™ / MINNEAPOLIS

To all seven of my grandchildren, from toddler to middle schoolers:
Jamie, Jackson, Lael, Judah, Hayley, Alethia, and Collin.
I write these books for you.

Twenty-First Century Books
An imprint of Lerner Publishing Group, Inc.
241 First Avenue North
Minneapolis, MN 55401 USA

For reading levels and more information, look up this title at www.lernerbooks.com.

Main body text set in Tw Cen Classified MT Std.
Typeface provided by Agfa.

Library of Congress Cataloging-in-Publication Data

Names: Miller, Michael, 1958– author.
Title: Cyberspies : inside the world of hacking, online privacy, and cyberterrorism / Michael Miller.
Description: Minneapolis, MN : Twenty-First Century Books, [2021] | Includes bibliographical references and index. | Audience: Ages: 11–18 | Audience: Grades: 7–9 | Summary: "As the digital world grows, teens must be aware of threats to their online privacy and security. This book details forms of cyberspying, explores careers in cyberintelligence, and looks at various online threats"— Provided by publisher.
Identifiers: LCCN 2020022338 (print) | LCCN 2020022339 (ebook) | ISBN 9781728413907 (library binding) | ISBN 9781728419091 (ebook)
Subjects: LCSH: Cyber intelligence (Computer security)—Juvenile literature.
Classification: LCC QA76.9.A25 M582 2021 (print) | LCC QA76.9.A25 (ebook) | DDC 005.8—dc23

LC record available at https://lccn.loc.gov/2020022338
LC ebook record available at https://lccn.loc.gov/2020022339

Manufactured in the United States of America
1-48543-49043-10/2/2020

Table of Contents

CHAPTER 1

SPIES LIKE US:
INSIDE THE WORLD OF CYBERINTELLIGENCE

The National Security Operations Center and other National Security Agency branches monitor threats to the United States. Many of those threats come via cyberspace.

Loren Sands-Ramshaw has always loved technology. Born in 1988, he grew up in the Washington, DC, area, the heart of the US government. Like many kids of his generation, he played video games for fun and used computers to connect with friends and do schoolwork. When he was eleven, the *Washington Post* included him in an article about tween buying habits. He told the reporter about his dream bedroom: "I would love my own computer, a TV, and a Nintendo 64 in my room. And a soft armchair to read in."

In high school at Sidwell Friends School in Bethesda, Maryland, Sands-Ramshaw loved math and science. He was a member of Sidwell's mathematics team, which competed against teams from other high schools to solve difficult math problems. After high school he attended Dartmouth College in Hanover, New Hampshire. He graduated magna cum laude (with great distinction) with a bachelor's degree in computer science. His honors thesis was about how terrorists might use the internet to attack the US power grid—the network of wires and equipment used to transmit electricity and other kinds of power across the nation.

After graduation, he was offered a job by the National Security Agency (NSA), part of the US Department of Defense (DOD). The NSA monitors, collects, and processes intelligence, or information about potential threats to the United States, from around the globe. It's a spy agency, and it wanted Sands-Ramshaw to join its team of US government cyberspies.

The NSA often works online. Its agents frequently hack computers, smartphones, and online networks to gather data. Sands-Ramshaw's background in math and computers made him an ideal candidate for the agency, which wanted to expand its base of tech-savvy employees. The agency was especially interested in people with a knowledge of malware (malicious software, including computer viruses), cryptography (breaking secret codes), and computer network security (defending networks from online attacks). Sands-Ramshaw easily met these requirements.

"I was a spy for the US government," he said about his new job. But he quickly discovered that NSA employees aren't spies in the way the fictional James Bond is a spy. They don't go on missions in enemy territory, they don't carry weapons and fancy spy gadgets, and they're never in physical danger. Instead, the agency's cyberspies work behind the scenes

Fictional spies such as James Bond use guns and other deadly weapons. Cyberspies, on the other hand, usually work in offices. Their tools are computers.

in a safe environment. They sit in front of computers, gathering and analyzing electronic intelligence from the internet. Working as an NSA spy is a desk job.

Many fictional spies operate outside the law. They lie, steal secret information, and double-cross enemy agents. But Sands-Ramshaw described his NSA coworkers as "law-abiding type[s]." They had to be, since all potential NSA employees go through rigid background checks, psychological screening, and polygraph (lie detector) tests. During the background check, an NSA agent calls all the personal and professional references a job candidate has listed and even walks around the job candidate's neighborhood or school and asks people about them. The psychological screening is designed to identify troubling personality traits, such as a tendency to lie or cheat. During the polygraph test, job applicants answer questions designed to determine if they are "law-abiding and patriotic." One question is,

"Have you ever given classified [secret government] information to a foreign entity?"

And all NSA job candidates have to fill out the government's Standard Form 86. This 127-page questionnaire asks applicants about their schooling; where they have lived, worked, and traveled; foreigners they've worked with or been friends with; and other life history. Then staffers with the agency verify that each answer to each question is true.

The application process is long and involved, but it's effective in weeding out unqualified and unsuitable job candidates. It is highly unlikely that any foreign spies or people with criminal backgrounds would make it past the screening.

Sands-Ramshaw said he was "impressed not only by [his fellow NSA employees'] technical ability, but also by their dedication to the mission. They are the most earnest and conscientious group of people I have ever met."

During his first year at the agency, Sands-Ramshaw worked close to home, at NSA headquarters in Fort Meade, Maryland. He was assigned to the agency's Computer Network Operations Development Program. His job title was global network vulnerability analyst. His job was to write code for computer systems that gather and manage electronic intelligence. Though not as thrilling as James Bond–style missions, it was vitally important. Somebody has to keep the NSA computer systems running.

His office was a small room in a bland building. It was much like any other office building in any other office park in any other city in the United States, except it was on a US Army base with extremely tight security. Like all the other rooms in the building, the office contained several desks, each with its own computer and monitor. Sands-Ramshaw did his coding there.

A typical day for Sands-Ramshaw and his colleagues involved developing, running, maintaining, and modifying computer software for the NSA. The software scooped up intelligence from phones and the internet, including emails, text messages, social media posts, and web pages generated by both foreign and US citizens. Other NSA employees analyzed this data, looking for potential threats to the United States.

Sands-Ramshaw worked for the NSA for two years, from 2010 to 2012. Since leaving the agency, he has written books about coding, developed websites and mobile apps, and blogged about his experiences inside and outside of the NSA. Of his time in the cyberintelligence industry, he writes, "If you are a US citizen, I hope you are reassured to know how capable and thorough your cyber spy agency and military command are. I was extremely impressed by the Agency's capabilities."

SPY VERSUS SPY

Traditional spy work involves collecting information about threats and enemies, analyzing that information, and sharing the information with those who need it. Cyberspying involves the same thing, only the collecting, analyzing, and sharing of information are done online and with computers. Cyberintelligence, then, blends modern information technology (IT) with traditional espionage.

US Cyber Command coordinates the cyberintelligence teams of each US military branch. These service members are part of a US Air Force cyberoperations unit.

HELP WANTED

What do US cyberspies think of their jobs? On Indeed.com, one wrote that the job was in "a demanding environment but you really felt like you were making a difference. The days were somewhat long but there was never a dull minute and you always had plenty to do. It was exciting and meaningful."

Another cyberspy wrote, "Never the same thing twice. Every day is a different challenge and opportunity to learn. Everyone has a chance to grow and learn in this environment."

But working in cyberintelligence, especially for the US government, is not for everyone. Some quit because of the stress and long hours. Some leave because they're frustrated with government bureaucracy. Others leave to take higher-paying jobs in private business. For example, General Keith Alexander was director of the NSA and head of Cyber Command from 2010 to 2014. He retired from the military to found his own firm, IronNet Cybersecurity. His company employs several other ex-government cyberspies.

This talent drain to the private sector is a problem for the government's cyberintelligence agencies. The NSA says that 8 to 9 percent of its cyberintelligence employees leave each year. Some groups within the NSA lose even more staff. Ellison Anne Williams, a former senior researcher at the NSA, said, "The agency is losing an amazing amount of its strongest technical talent, and to lose your best and brightest staff is a huge hit." She says that the private cyberintelligence firm she founded, Enveil, recruited at least ten employees from the NSA.

Despite the brain drain to the private sector, the NSA still attracts and retains skilled technical talent. NSA head Paul Nakasone says that the agency receives seventeen thousand employment applications each month. The NSA has earned multiple honors for being an excellent employer. Many job applicants are inspired by patriotism. When recruiting employees, Nakasone says, "Our mission sells itself. We are defending our nation."

Cyperspies play both defense and offense. Defensively, they try to learn about threats posed by foreign enemies, terrorist groups, and criminal organizations. The information that cyberspies gather can help defend a nation against attacks. But the attackers don't use only guns, bombs, and armies anymore. They also conduct cyberattacks—infiltrating computer systems to steal information and to disable electronic networks that run military, government, business, and industrial operations. So cyberspies must defend against those kinds of attacks too. Offensively, cyberspies launch cyberattacks of their own: they infiltrate enemy computer networks to steal secret information or to disable enemy business or military operations.

The NSA is just one of several US government agencies that employ cyberspies. The Central Intelligence Agency (CIA), Department of Homeland Security (DHS), Federal Bureau of Investigation (FBI), and other government agencies each employ thousands of cyberintelligence professionals.

The United States Cyber Command, created in 2009, unifies the formerly separate cyberunits of the US Air Force, US Army, US Marine Corps, and US Navy. It is based in Fort Meade, Maryland, near the headquarters of the NSA. Cyber Command is tasked with defending DOD computers from cyberattacks, providing cyberintelligence to US military commanders around the globe, and helping the US government detect, thwart, and respond to cyberattacks.

OPERATION GLOWING SYMPHONY

While it was originally a strictly defensive organization, Cyber Command has since added offensive capabilities. This means it can support and even participate in combat missions against US enemies. For example, in 2015 Cyber Command joined with the NSA to attack the terrorist group known as the Islamic State in Iraq and Syria (ISIS). Based in the Middle East, ISIS aims to build a society rooted in an extreme interpretation of the Islamic religion. The group is known for its brutal acts, including beheadings, mass shootings, bombings, and other acts of terror. The US cybermission, dubbed Operation Glowing

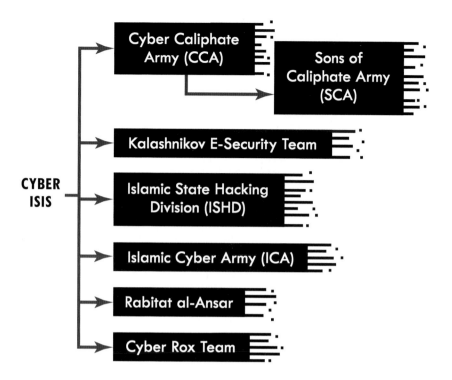

CYBER ISIS
- Cyber Caliphate Army (CCA)
- Sons of Caliphate Army (SCA)
- Kalashnikov E-Security Team
- Islamic State Hacking Division (ISHD)
- Islamic Cyber Army (ICA)
- Rabitat al-Ansar
- Cyber Rox Team

ISIS runs a multilevel cyberterrorism program, composed of at least seven branches. The United States has countered ISIS with cyberattacks of its own, including Operation Glowing Symphony in 2016.

Symphony, had the goal of disrupting ISIS's cyberspace operations. The plan was to hack into and disable computer servers running the terrorist organization's websites, online magazine, and smartphone app.

The US cyberattack started with a series of phishing emails. Phishing scams are designed to trick users into disclosing personal information, such as passwords, which can then be used to log into secure computer networks. The US cyberspies sent email messages to key players in ISIS, encouraging them to click on links in the emails. The phishing emails were designed to resemble official ISIS messages, complete with official logos. The links within the emails led to equally phony websites, where unsuspecting users were encouraged to enter usernames and passwords.

As head of the NSA, General Paul Nakasone led Operation Glowing Symphony and other cyberattacks against US enemies.

All the cyberspies needed was a single recipient of a phishing email to unknowingly enter login information. That would give the US spies access to ISIS's IT systems. The Americans tricked several recipients into clicking on the phony links and entering their usernames and passwords.

The Cyber Command experts were then inside the ISIS computer network. There they created backdoors, or ways to bypass the site's normal cybersecurity measures. The spies could use these doors to easily enter the system again at any time.

Once inside the ISIS network, the US spies started searching for critical data and materials. They took screenshots of secret ISIS documents. Then they started disrupting the system. They deleted files and folders. They changed users' passwords. They locked ISIS administrators out of their own accounts. They installed malware that could be triggered later to cause even more damage. "Within the first 60 minutes . . . I knew we were having success," said Nakasone, "We would see the targets [ISIS online communications and networks] start to come down."

Operation Glowing Symphony made life very difficult for ISIS. Dabiq, ISIS's online magazine, started missing publication deadlines.

Some of the organization's websites crashed and never came back up. The group's smartphone app stopped working. Communications were disrupted. The operation was a success.

This spy work was all conducted by Cyber Command staff from the comfort and safety of their computers at Fort Meade headquarters. In carrying out Operation Glowing Symphony, nobody at Cyber Command was in danger, nobody got hurt, and nobody missed lunch. No gunshots were fired. The only sounds were of fingers tapping at keyboards. For the cyberspies of Cyber Command, it was just another day at the office.

CYBERSLEUTHING:
SEARCHING FOR INFORMATION (LEGALLY)

This ship's manifest provides names, ages, and other details about slaves transported to North America in the early 1800s. Amateur cybersleuths who want to learn about their ancestors can find this type of information online.

Brett Miller knew that some of his ancestors had lived in Tennessee during the nineteenth century. But he wanted to know about earlier generations of ancestors, so he launched an online search. He turned to Ancestry, FamilyTreeNow, Genealogy.com, and other websites that help people trace their ancestry. Depending on where your ancestors are from, these websites can help you research your family history. The sites contain many historical public documents, including birth and death certificates, marriage certificates, census records, and draft records from the United States and some other countries. Users can search through these documents to find clues about their ancestors' lives. Many searchers who've successfully uncovered information about their ancestors post it on the genealogy websites for others to use. This user-generated data helps distant family members connect and fill out their own family trees.

Brett Miller's online research led him from Tennessee in the nineteenth century back through many earlier generations of family members. He discovered that one of his ancestors was Monzongo Montsingaux, who was born around 1580 in the southwestern African nation of Angola. In 1610 Montsingaux and his wife Nzinga Mbande had a son named Duarte. During a war in 1622, Portuguese slave traders captured Duarte and brought him to the colony of Virginia in North America. There Duarte, with the spelling of his last name changed to Mozingo, worked for no wages under a labor practice known as indentured servitude. His master was a wealthy man named John Walker. In colonial Virginia at this time, many Black and white workers were indentured servants. White servants became free after working for their masters for a certain number of years, usually four or seven. But Mozingo was Black, and Black indentured servants did not become free after a period of years. They were slaves by another name.

Brett learned that Duarte's son Edward Mozingo was born in 1644. Edward also worked as an indentured servant, first for Walker and then for John Stone, another wealthy Virginian. Edward Mozingo made history in 1672 by becoming the first Black man in Virginia to go to court and win his freedom from indentured servitude.

Brett Miller's family members were intrigued to learn about their African ancestors. Most of their other ancestors were white Europeans. Brett's online sleuthing uncovered a previously unknown branch of the family tree and opened a window to the struggles of Black people in colonial North America.

Brett Miller's online ancestry research was a form of cybersleuthing. Cybersleuths don't hack into or attack computer systems as cyberspies do. Cybersleuths simply search online for publicly available information. They use search engines, websites, and databases to find the information they're looking for—and don't break any laws doing so. They're a lot like old-school private detectives, but they do their work in front of computer screens.

DIGITAL PRIVATE EYES

Cybersleuthing is common. Many people do online searches to find contact information for old friends they've lost touch with. In the business world, human resources staff members often use cybersleuthing to find background information on job applicants. Before an election, candidates sometimes hire cybersleuths to dig up negative information about political opponents. Or, like Brett Miller, cybersleuths might search online to build their family trees. Anybody can be a cybersleuth. All you need is a computer and an internet connection.

The internet is a practically infinite source of information about almost everything. Want to find out where someone went to school? Look online. Want to see the financial history of a particular company? Google it. Want to learn more about a given topic or profession? Search the web. Want to know more about a person you're thinking of dating? Do an image search.

Some information is hiding in plain sight, available with a simple search with Google or another search engine. Some information is found on LinkedIn and other career-oriented websites. Other information is stored in topic-specific databases, on corporate websites, or in newspaper archives. Some information is free to searchers. Other information can be accessed only by members of a certain professional organization or by those who pay a subscription fee. Here are some of the more popular places to search:

- Search engines. Google, Bing, and other search engines are the first places cybersleuths look when they're researching a person, company, event, or other topic. Google Images allows users to upload a person's picture to find other pictures of that person. These pictures might be linked to additional information, such as the person's name or address.
- Social media. People of all ages and interests hang out on Facebook, Twitter, Instagram, and other social media sites. Many people include a lot of personal information and photos in their social media profiles. Some people upload personal videos to YouTube, so that's a good place to look. LinkedIn is another source of both professional and personal information. There, users can often find out where a person works, lives, and more.
- People search sites. These are sites designed specifically to help searchers find individuals, and most are free. Popular people search sites include AnyWho, PeopleFinders, Spokeo, and True People Search. They provide basic information, such as the person's age, address, and family members' names. Users usually have to pay to get more specific information, such as whether that person has ever been arrested.
- Alumni sites. If you know where a person went to high school or college, you can find out more by searching alumni sites such as Alumni.NET and Classmates. Many high schools and colleges also have searchable alumni pages or websites.
- Obituary and tribute sites. If you're looking for someone who has died, you can check out obituary and tribute sites, such

as Legacy.com and Tributes.com. These sites post information from newspaper obituaries and funeral homes.

- Government records. The internet makes it relatively easy to find out if a person has ever been arrested, gone bankrupt, or had other legal troubles. Some of this information is accessible on state and local government websites. For a fee, the Public Record Research System offers online searching of

WEBSLEUTHING: WATCHING THE DETECTIVES

Have you ever watched a true crime TV show or listened to a true crime podcast and said to yourself, "I could solve this case"? A number of cybersleuths have done just that. These websleuths work on their own or team up with law enforcement to dig up clues about unsolved cases.

Take, for example, the case of the anonymous woman whose body was found in the small city of Georgetown, Kentucky, in 1968. Medical experts said the woman was a little over 5 feet (1.5 m) tall, weighed about 110 pounds (50 kg), and had reddish-brown hair. The media called her Tent Girl, referring to the tarp in which her body was wrapped, but the police were unable to determine her real identity or who killed her.

Thirty years later, in 1998, cybersleuth Todd Matthews helped break the case. Matthews was the son-in-law of Wilbur Riddle, the man who discovered Tent Girl's body. Matthews had been fascinated with the case for years and used his free time to scour the internet for information. One evening he happened across a profile on a missing persons website that matched the description of the dead woman. He passed the information onto the missing woman's sister in Arkansas, who in turn contacted the local police in Kentucky. Authorities dug up Tent Girl's body and

court and government records. You can also look up federal court records through the Public Access to Court Electronic Records website.
- Newspaper and magazine archives. Most local and national newspapers, as well as online and print magazines, maintain searchable online archives and databases. Some of these sources are free, but many require a paid subscription.

conducted a DNA test (an analysis of chemical markers in cells that are unique to each person). The test revealed that Tent Girl was in fact the missing woman, Barbara Ann "Bobbie" Taylor. When she died, she was a twenty-three-year-old housewife from Lexington, Kentucky, and the mother of an eight-month-old daughter. Taylor's husband, George Earl Taylor, hadn't filed a missing person report at the time, instead telling her family that Bobbie had run off with another man.

Matthews's work led the police to identify George Earl Taylor as the prime suspect in his wife's murder. But he died of cancer in 1987. However, Todd Matthews went on to help build the Doe Network (named after the names John Doe and Jane Doe, used to identify unknown crime victims), an online database that contains information on more than three thousand missing person cases.

Websleuths have used the Doe Network and other online sources, such as the DOJ's National Missing and Unidentified Persons System (NamUs) database, to solve other cold cases. NamUs claims to have helped solve more than two thousand missing persons cases and identify more than fifteen hundred previously unidentified bodies since the site was launched in 2007. The Doe Network says it has helped close ninety cases.

CORPORATE CYBERSLEUTHING

Sleuthing has long been a part of the corporate world. Businesses want to know what their competitors are up to. With enough information about a competing business, such as its annual sales figures, leadership changes, and product plans, a company can tweak its own products and marketing campaigns to beat the competition. For example, suppose a company, through perfectly legal cybersleuthing, discovers that a rival company is planning a new TV, radio, and web ad campaign. The sleuthing company might then create its own ad campaign and launch it before the competitor launches its own. By getting its ads online and over the airwaves first, the cybersleuthing company might be able to lure customers away from the competitor.

Not surprisingly, much corporate information is available on the internet. Corporate researchers scour public and subscription databases in search of useful industry information, including about their competitors. As with all cybersleuthing, much information is available from simple Google searches, while finding other data requires a deeper dive. Many corporations subscribe to business-focused databases and news services, including D&B Hoovers, IBISWorld, MarketResearch.com, and PRWeb.

WHEN CYBERSLEUTHING GOES TOO FAR

When cybersleuthing becomes excessive, it can turn into cyberstalking. Some cyberstalkers follow their victims online, sometimes just lurking in the background on social media sites and sometimes making threatening or rude comments on the victim's posts. Some cyberstalkers monitor location-tagged social media posts and photos, find their victims in the real world, and harass them in person. Some use malware to take over victims' webcams and then spy on them through their computers. Sexual predators often use some or all of these techniques to get close to unsuspecting victims.

Cyberbullying and doxing are forms of cyberstalking. Cyberbullying involves using email and online forums to send threatening or hurtful messages to a victim. Doxing is when a stalker posts private information

When Professor Christine Blasey Ford testified against Supreme Court nominee Brett Kavanaugh, his supporters attacked and threatened her online. Such attacks are against the law.

about a victim, such as an address and phone number, and encourages others to use this information to harass the victim. University professor Christine Blasey Ford became a doxing victim in 2019 when she accused US Supreme Court nominee Brett Kavanaugh of sexual assault. Supporters of Kavanaugh posted Ford's home address, email address, and phone number on Twitter, which led to a barrage of harassing messages and threats that forced Ford to abandon her home.

Cyberstalking is against the law. As of 2020, fourteen US states had made cyberstalking and related activities a criminal offense. The federal government has outlawed cyberstalking through the 2013 Violence Against Women Reauthorization Act and other legislation. If you find yourself the victim of any form of cyberstalking, avoid engaging with the stalker. Block all the stalker's messages. Change all your social media passwords, and ask social networks to remove any offensive posts. If the stalking persists, report it to your parents, teachers, school counselors, or law enforcement. Don't feel embarrassed or try to hide what's happening. It's not your fault. Confide in authority figures for support and advice. You can report cyberstalking and find out more at Fight Cyberstalking (www.fightcyberstalking.org) and the Cyberbullying Research Center (www.cyberbullying.org/cyberstalking).

CYBERSLEUTHS IN LOVE

Thinking about cybersleuthing to learn about a potential date? Chances are, that person is cybersleuthing you too! According to the background screening company JDP, 61 percent of people always or usually research their potential partners before going on a first date. Facebook is the most popular resource, used by 88 percent of dating cybersleuths. Google is also popular, used by 70 percent of people surveyed. Instagram is used by 53 percent of respondents, and Twitter and LinkedIn are used by 21 percent each. LeslieBeth Wish, psychotherapist and founder of the LoveVictory website, says, "Healthy research includes looking at the person's tweets and [social media] profiles. You can learn about their interests, accomplishments, goals, and education or training."

HOW OFTEN PEOPLE RESEARCH POTENTIAL DATES

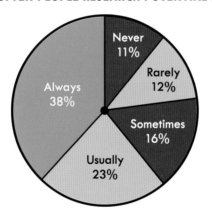

It's possible to take research on potential partners too far, however. For example, a man named Steve noticed a woman who called herself Pianobaby on an online dating site. Steve liked her profile but wanted to find out more before contacting her. By downloading her photo into Google Images, he found her profile on other websites. That way he discovered Pianobaby's real name (Julie), where she grew up, where she had gone to college, and what she did for a living. He visited Julie's personal and professional websites and watched some videos she'd uploaded to YouTube. He discovered her favorite restaurants, the type of music she liked, and a lot more. He even found her mailing address and phone number. Instead of contacting Julie through the online dating site, Steve surprised her with a personal phone call. He started talking about her interests, where she'd lived and visited, and other personal details he'd learned from his online research. He meant the information to be a conversation starter, but Julie just found it creepy. She was not happy about Steve's online sleuthing and didn't accept his offer of a date.

Without being as invasive as Steve, you can still learn about a potential date ahead of time to weed out bad matches and possible trouble. Sometimes online searches reveal that a potential date is already married or in another relationship. Searches might also show that a possible romantic interest has a criminal history. As Bela Gandhi, founder and CEO of Chicago-based Smart Dating Academy, says, "Research is a big part of having fun and staying safe. . . . You want to make sure this person is authentic; so people are doing research to make sure what they see is what they get."

WHERE PEOPLE CONDUCT RESEARCH ON POTENTIAL DATES

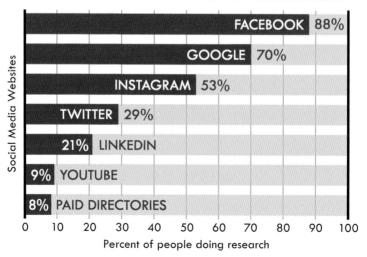

Social Media Websites

- FACEBOOK 88%
- GOOGLE 70%
- INSTAGRAM 53%
- TWITTER 29%
- 21% LINKEDIN
- 9% YOUTUBE
- 8% PAID DIRECTORIES

0 10 20 30 40 50 60 70 80 90 100

Percent of people doing research

CHAPTER 3

CYBERESPIONAGE:
OBTAINING SECRET INFORMATION

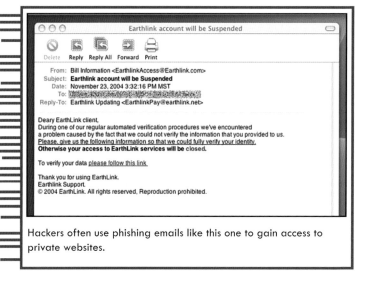

Hackers often use phishing emails like this one to gain access to private websites.

During the 2017 and 2018 school years, universities around the globe found themselves the target of cyberspies. Hackers were stealing unpublished research, manuscripts, and other materials from their online libraries.

The operation was simple. Professors, staff, and students at the targeted institutions received official-looking emails that appeared to be from the university or the university library. These emails said that the recipients needed to reactivate their library accounts and included a link to do so. When a recipient clicked on the link, they were taken to a web page that looked almost identical to the official home page of the university library site.

The web pages, however, were "spoofed." They were totally fake, created by cyberspies to obtain the recipients' login credentials: usernames and passwords. With that information, the cyberspies could log into the targeted library websites and download valuable subscription-only research and other data. Some of the data concerned top-secret government projects. Other data involved valuable scientific research.

The hacking operation was global. The cyberspies targeted seventy-six universities and research institutions in fourteen countries, including the United States, Canada, Australia, China, Israel, and Japan. Another forty-seven private companies in the United States and abroad were also targeted, as well as the US Department of Labor and the United Nations. The operation involved three hundred spoofed websites.

Cybersecurity experts named the hacking group Cobalt Dickens and traced it to Iran's Islamic Revolutionary Guard Corps, a branch of the Iranian armed forces. Following an attack in 2017 by the same group, the DOJ had charged nine Iranians with the cybertheft of more than 31 terabytes of data—the equivalent of more than two billion pages of text. The 2018 operation was likely a continuation of the previous attack. "The hackers targeted innovations and intellectual property [ideas, systems, and inventions] from our country's greatest minds," said Geoffrey Berman, a federal government attorney. Rafe Pilling of Secureworks, the firm that discovered the breach, thinks that the hackers hope to sell the information they stole.

The Cobalt Dickens hackers didn't stop in 2018. In August 2019 researchers discovered a new phishing campaign from Cobalt Dickens, again aimed at universities in the United States and around the world. Although cybersecurity experts have identified the cybercriminals, the attacks continue.

BEYOND CYBERSLEUTHING

Whereas cybersleuthing involves legal online digging, cyberespionage goes one step beyond. In cyberespionage, cyberspies use online tools to illegally obtain government and business secrets. Cyberespionage operations can be used for economic, political, or military benefit.

The Merriam-Webster dictionary defines espionage as "the practice of spying or using spies to obtain information about the plans and activities especially of a foreign government or a competing company." Those who engage in cyberespionage employ computers and the internet to conduct these activities.

The history of cyberespionage dates to the 1980s. In one example, in 1986, West German hacker Markus Hess accessed computers at various US military bases. He was looking for military secrets that he could sell to the KGB, the spy agency of the former Soviet Union. This nation, based in Russia, was then a long-standing enemy of the United States. Clifford Stoll, a systems administrator at Lawrence Berkeley National Laboratory in California, which does research for the military, discovered the intrusion. Stoll noticed unusual activity in the lab's computers and set a trap for the hacker. He created what cybersecurity experts call a honeypot. It was a computer server containing a store of enticing but fake data—and Hess didn't know it was fake. When Hess accessed the server (via a dial-up telephone line), Stoll was able to trace his phone number and pass the information on to law enforcement. West German authorities arrested Hess, found the fake data on his computer, and convicted him of cybercrimes.

In 1996 a group of hackers, believed to be working for the Russian government, began a yearslong cyber infiltration of a variety of US government agencies. Targets included the US Navy, the US Air Force, the DOD, National Aeronautics and Space Administration (NASA), and several military bases. The hackers established backdoors to allow them to reenter the organizations' computer systems at any time. They not only stole classified information but also installed software that rerouted network traffic from the compromised computer servers to Russia. The investigation into this episode, dubbed Moonlight Maze, estimated that if all the stolen data were to be printed out and stacked, it would reach a height of 1,665 feet (507 m)—three times the height of the Washington Monument.

Cyberespionage became even more common after the turn of the twenty-first century, as more and more business communication moved online. In 2009 a team of hackers carried out hundreds of cyberattacks against a variety of US businesses. Cybersecurity experts named the event Operation Aurora and determined that the Chinese government was behind the attacks. One target was Google's computer servers, where the attackers found information about Chinese spies who were under surveillance (being watched) by US authorities. The hackers also accessed the Gmail accounts of Chinese human rights activists—people who spoke out against the repressive Chinese government. And the attackers stole trade secrets (such as product designs, marketing plans, and manufacturing practices) from Adobe, Northrop Grumman, Symantec, and at least thirty other US companies.

A group of hackers employed by the government of North Korea carried out a cyberattack on the film production company Sony Pictures in November 2014. These hackers, calling themselves the Guardians of Peace, acted in response to Sony's planned release of the movie comedy The Interview, which they believed was disrespectful to North Korean leader Kim Jong-un. (Sony subsequently decided not to release the film into theaters, although it did come out on DVD.)

The Sony attack was twofold. First, the hackers infiltrated Sony's computer network and copied a large amount of confidential data. This data included salary information, private email communications about movies and employees, scripts of not-yet-released films, and plans for future films. The group then leaked this data to the public, exposing behind-the-scenes politics and gossip and generally disrupting company operations. The second part of the attack involved releasing a variant of the powerful Shamoon malware into Sony's computer network. The malware erased the hard drives of individual PCs and servers, and took the entire company network off-line for several days, totally disrupting normal operations.

Following the Sony hack, US president Barack Obama said that the United States would have a "proportional response" to the attack. US government cybersecurity departments act in secret, so no one knew for sure what the response would be. But a month later, all of North Korea lost its connection to the internet for more than ten hours. Was the United States behind this disruption? If so, US government cyberspies are not admitting to it.

Angered by the comedy film *The Interview*, North Korean hackers attacked Sony Pictures with powerful malware in 2014.

SOCIAL ENGINEERING

Social engineering is the practice of manipulating people, often using trickery. Cyberspies frequently use social engineering. For example, on the phone or via email, a cyberspy might lie to a company help desk employee to fraudulently obtain computer login credentials.

Phishing and spear phishing are common social engineering techniques. Phishing scams are designed to trick users into disclosing personal information, such as passwords, which can then be used to log into secure computer networks. In a phishing attack, cybercriminals send large numbers of an identical email, hoping that a few or even just one of the recipients will fall for the scam. In a spear phishing attack, the email is tailored to one particular victim, which makes it even more likely to succeed.

One instance of spear phishing occurred in February 2020. The victim was businesswoman Barbara Corcoran, a star of the TV show *Shark Tank*. The perpetrator assumed the online persona of Corcoran's personal assistant and used an email address that differed from Corcoran's real assistant's email address by one letter. Then the perpetrator sent an email to Corcoran's bookkeeper, instructing her to pay $388,700.11 to a German company named Ffh Concept GmbH. The bookkeeper responded, asking what the money was for. The spear phisher responded by saying it was for designing some German apartment units in which Corcoran had invested. The whole thing looked legitimate to the bookkeeper, who authorized the payment. The spear phisher had done research, finding out the name and email addresses of Corcoran's assistant and bookkeeper and learning that Corcoran had invested in German real estate. The spear phisher also knew that Ffh Concept GmbH was a real German company. The account to which the bookkeeper sent the funds, however, belonged to the spear phisher.

When Corcoran's real assistant found out about the payment, she realized that Corcoran had been scammed. Corcoran's IT staff traced the phishing emails to a server in China. Corcoran's staff also contacted the German bank being used to transfer the funds. That bank stopped the payment before it went through to China, saving Corcoran from losing nearly $400,000 to spear phishers.

STEALING CORPORATE SECRETS

Cyberespionage isn't the sole province of government intelligence agencies. Sometimes private criminal organizations do the spying. For example, in the 2010s, a group of private hackers called Butterfly infiltrated a number of multibillion-dollar technology corporations, including Apple, Facebook, Microsoft, and Twitter. The group used its own suite of custom malware tools to steal high-level corporate information, which could be sold to the highest bidder. Cyberexperts still don't know who was behind the Butterfly attacks.

Cyberespionage in the corporate world is often used to steal trade secrets, such as recipes for popular food products and technical details about manufacturing and equipment. Companies can then make similar or superior products to those offered by a competitor. In September 2019, European aerospace company Airbus disclosed that it had been hit by a series of cyberespionage attacks. Cyberspies had infiltrated several of the company's subcontractors (parts suppliers), including jet engine—maker Rolls-Royce, to obtain commercial secrets. The hackers were looking for technical documents related to different parts of aircraft manufactured by Airbus, especially the planes' propulsion systems. Because the attackers used advanced technological tools to cover their tracks, Airbus was unable to identify who did the hacking, although they suspected that Chinese companies were involved.

The Center for Strategic and International Studies estimates that cyberespionage costs the global economy close to $600 billion a year. This figure includes the cost of stolen intellectual property and business downtime caused by cyberattacks.

STEALING GOVERNMENT SECRETS

Cyberespionage is an important weapon for most countries' military and spy agencies. Governments use cyberespionage to spy on other countries, steal military secrets, and attack computer networks. Sometimes the targets are other governments, and sometimes the targets are terrorist organizations or dangerous individuals. The

Commercial documents, such as plans for building airplanes and other vehicles, can be worth millions of dollars. Hackers attack corporate websites to steal this kind of valuable data.

techniques are always the same: gain access to secure computer networks with the intent of stealing confidential information and sometimes disrupting operations.

One of the more famous cases of government-backed cyberespionage was dubbed Titan Rain. This operation, which occurred from 2003 to 2007, involved Chinese hackers who infiltrated a number of government agencies in the United States and the United Kingdom. They targeted the FBI, NASA, and the US Departments of Energy, Homeland Security, and State, as well as the United Kingdom's Foreign Office and Ministry of Defence. The operation also targeted several manufacturers that provide weapons and vehicles to the US military.

Titan Rain was a state-sponsored attack—the hackers worked for the People's Liberation Army, the armed forces of China. The goal of Titan Rain was to obtain sensitive information, including military secrets, from secure government servers. The ongoing attacks were

PROBLEMS WITH PRIVATE CONTRACTORS

Not all US government cyberspies are directly employed by the federal government. Instead, they work for private contractors, such as Booz Allen Hamilton, General Dynamics, Hewlett Packard, IBM, and Northrup Grumman. The US government hires such firms to handle part of its cybersecurity work. But private contractors can present their own security risks. Their employees often work in government offices, but they don't always go through the same rigorous vetting process the government uses for its own employees. That can open the door to security leaks. The most famous example involved Edward Snowden. Snowden, then employed by Booz Allen Hamilton, worked as an IT administrator at an NSA office in Hawaii. There he obtained secret documents about a US government effort to spy on US citizens. Snowden later gave the documents to reporters. Since that event, both the federal government and its contractors have tightened rules for the screening of cybersecurity employees.

Another problem with private contractors is that they make attractive targets for enterprising hackers. Smaller firms especially often do not have the same level of security as larger contractors and the government itself. Hackers can exploit small vulnerabilities at these firms to gain access to larger government systems. For example, in early 2018 hackers from the Chinese government breached the computers of an unnamed contractor working with the Naval Undersea Warfare Center, part of the US Navy. The hackers stole data related to a secret navy project known as Sea Dragon, as well as vast amounts of other military information. The data was stored on the contractor's own computer network, which was inadequately protected from cyberthreats.

not designed to cause damage to the compromised networks. Indeed, the hackers made sure not to disrupt the networks' normal operation, so they could stay hidden and return over and over again to abscond with even more secrets.

Each individual attack started with the hackers scanning the targeted computer system, looking for vulnerabilities in system security. Next, the attackers used phishing and other tricks to obtain users' login credentials. Once inside the targeted system, the hackers installed a backdoor, which could be opened at a later date to gain further access. The hackers took care to remain undetected so that they could maintain a persistent presence and thus steal data at their leisure.

Cybersecurity experts first discovered Titan Rain in 2005, and it took several years for the US and UK governments to fully secure systems and shut down the ongoing attacks. Not surprisingly, Titan Rain increased existing tensions between the United States and China. Many officials saw China's cyberespionage as the beginning of a cyberwar between China and the West (the industrialized nations of Europe and North America).

CHAPTER 4

CYBERPOLITICS:
HACKING THE VOTE

To protect voting systems from cyberattacks in 2018, the State of Washington worked with cybersecurity experts from the Washington Air National Guard.

Politics can be a cutthroat business, and part of that business is digging up dirt on political rivals. The goals of this opposition research are to find out as much as possible about opposing candidates and to use that information to attack or embarrass them, making them look bad in the eyes of voters.

Many candidates hire consultants to work as cybersleuths on their behalf. The consultants search the internet for things the opposing candidate has said or written in the past. They sift through years of social media posts, looking for anything that might prove useful. They access all available online records, including government records. They try to find material that they can use against the opposition.

Veteran political consultant Alan Huffman details how he approaches online opposition research for his clients: "Initially we just start doing manic googling and find out everything that we can about them. Then we'll do an exhaustive LexisNexis [legal database] search and see what's been published. . . . If you're an incumbent [officeholder who's running for reelection], we're going to look at, what is your voting history [whether an official supported a certain law, for example], what comments have you made that are telling in any way. And we're going to look at whether you pay your taxes. Sometimes that leads you to interesting places."

CROSSING THE LEGAL LINE

Searching through public records to find dirt on a political opponent is perfectly legal. But throughout history, politicians have also conducted illegal opposition research as well. An infamous example is the Watergate scandal, which took place during the 1972 US presidential election. Designed to help President Richard Nixon win reelection, the scandal involved a number of crimes. Most notably, Republican operatives broke into the offices of the Democratic

National Committee, housed in the Watergate apartment and office buildings in Washington, DC, to steal information about Democratic presidential candidates. This was simple, old-fashioned espionage—and it was illegal. When the break-in and other Republican crimes came to light, President Richard Nixon resigned from office.

In the 1970s, President Richard Nixon and his allies tried to steal political secrets by breaking into a locked office. In the twenty-first century, political espionage usually takes place online instead.

In the twenty-first century, political espionage is more likely to be conducted online. Sometimes the cyberespionage consists of one candidate or party spying on another. Just as often, however, political cyberespionage is initiated by foreign players hoping to influence an election. In 2019 alone, officials reported more than eight hundred instances of cyberespionage against political parties and campaigns around the world. During the November 2019 elections in the United Kingdom, for example, cyberattackers hit the computers of both the Conservative and Labour Parties.

Tom Burt, head of customer security and trust for Microsoft, says that most political cyberattacks follow a similar pattern: "Early on in election cycles, we often see the majority of attacks targeting NGOs [nongovernment organizations] and think tanks involved in policy-making process and that are in communication with campaigns. As we get closer to elections themselves, we often see more attacks targeting campaigns themselves and the personal emails of campaign staff."

Hans Keirstead, a Democratic candidate for Congress from California, was the victim of one such cyberespionage operation. The operation began in August 2017 when cyberspies sent Keirstead a fake email that looked like an official Microsoft Office message.

HACKTIVISTS

Hacktivists are political activists who use hacking to advance their political agendas. They sometimes call themselves hackers with a cause. Their tactics include defacing websites, plastering message boards with their own messages, launching cyberattacks against organizations they dislike, and doxing politicians and officials they oppose.

One of the largest hacktivist groups in operation is called Anonymous. First appearing in 2003, Anonymous (whose members are, not surprisingly, anonymous) has launched attacks on a variety of targets in support of a variety of causes. For example, in 2011 Anonymous supported the Arab Spring populist uprisings in Middle Eastern countries by attacking government websites in Egypt and Tunisia, where officials were trying to suppress the uprisings. In February 2020 the group hacked the United Nations website and created a new page there for the island of Taiwan. The hacking was a symbolic action, meant to support the movement for Taiwan's independence from China. By creating a web page for Taiwan, Anonymous promoted the idea that Taiwan should be a self-governing country recognized by the United Nations. UN site administrators quickly took down Anonymous's Taiwan page.

This spear phishing email tricked Keirstead into entering his email password. The candidate quickly realized the message was fake and notified system administrators to secure the affected email system. Fortunately, their response was fast enough that no unauthorized access was made.

The operation continued in December of that year with a massive attack on the website and web server of Keirstead's campaign. Multiple hackers tried to log on to the network using hundreds of thousands of computer-generated username—password combinations over a two-and-a-half-month period. If the hackers happened on the right combination, they would have gotten access to the campaign's server. The attackers also tried to access the campaign's Twitter account. None of these attempts were successful.

Cybersecurity experts say that this cyberespionage could have been conducted by an organized crime group, a hacktivist group with a political agenda, or an interested foreign country. Russia was a prime suspect, as incumbent Representative Dana Rohrabacher is known for supporting Russia's military and policy positions. So hackers with ties to the Russian government might have acted to help keep Rohrabacher in office. The hackers never successfully infiltrated Keirstead's campaign, and he went on to lose in the primary, so he didn't face Rohrabacher in the general election.

THE RUSSIANS ARE COMING

One of the most notable instances of political espionage involved the 2016 US presidential election, in which Republican Donald Trump defeated Democrat Hillary Clinton. Before the election, Russian-based cyberspies hacked into the computer network of the Democratic National Committee (DNC). The attacks started with spear phishing emails to obtain usernames and passwords from DNC staffers. The groups thus gained access to the DNC's email server and subsequently stole thousands of emails and other documents stored there. The hackers released the stolen emails to the WikiLeaks organization. WikiLeaks released them to the news media.

US government investigators found that the cyberespionage groups involved had strong ties to the Russian government. The groups, known as APT28 and APT29 (also known as Fancy Bear and Cozy Bear, respectively), had been active since at least 2010. Both groups originally engaged in traditional espionage, targeting governments and military groups in the United States and Europe, but they eventually transitioned to cyberoperations.

Russian interference in the US election was not limited to the DNC hacking. The Russians also ran a massive disinformation campaign designed to confuse and mislead the American public. Disinformation is false information spread deliberately to influence public opinion or to hide the truth. A young Russian man, dubbed Maxim or Max by reporters, explained how the Russians carried out this campaign during the run-up to the 2016 US election.

Max graduated from Saint Petersburg State University in Russia and took a job with the Internet Research Agency (IRA). He worked there for a year and a half, in 2014–2015. The IRA is devoted to disseminating propaganda (information spread to further a cause or political belief) on behalf of Russian politicians and businesses. US intelligence officials believe the IRA was behind much of the Russian interference in the 2016 US presidential election.

FAKE ACCOUNT TWEETS AND RETWEETS ABOUT THE 2016 PRESIDENTIAL ELECTION

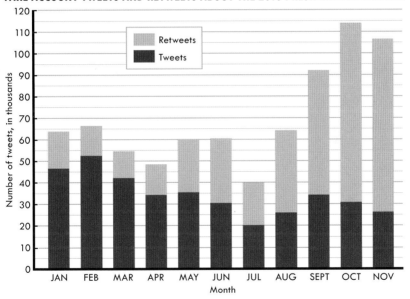

In the run-up to the US presidential election in 2016, Russia's Internet Research Agency created thousands of fake accounts on Twitter and other social media sites. The IRA used these accounts to flood US cyberspace with false and biased information about the presidential race. This chart shows the vast number of tweets and retweets from fake IRA Twitter accounts in 2016.

Before the election, the IRA assessed which of the major US candidates would be best for Russian business and political interests. It determined that Donald Trump's policies would be more favorable to Russia than would those of Hillary Clinton, so it geared its activities to helping Trump win the election.

Max says that the IRA was divided into two primary sections, a Russian desk and a foreign desk. Each department had about two hundred employees. On the Russian desk, employees set up fake and automated social media accounts on sites such as Facebook and Twitter. These robotic accounts, or bots, then posted and reposted fake news stories and pro-Trump propaganda.

WIKILEAKS

WikiLeaks, a nonprofit organization based in Iceland, is dedicated to publishing news leaks and classified information provided by anonymous sources. While WikiLeaks does not itself engage in hacking, it often publishes information obtained by hackers. The organization claims to have released ten million leaked documents in its first ten years of operation, including classified US military documents related to wars in Afghanistan, Iraq, and Yemen. WikiLeaks has released emails stolen by Russian hackers from Hillary Clinton's private email server when she was the US Secretary of State, as well as emails stolen from the Democratic National Committee during the 2016 presidential election.

The founder of WikiLeaks, Australian Julian Assange, believes that his organization is fighting injustice by revealing government and military misdeeds. But many others see WikiLeaks as a criminal organization. The US government has charged Assange with crimes for helping Chelsea Manning, a former US Army intelligence analyst, steal secret military documents.

The foreign desk, where Max worked, had a more complicated assignment. Its employees were tasked with stirring up discontent and divisiveness among US voters. Max and his coworkers learned about political issues in the United States, such as "tax problems, the problem of gays, sexual minorities, weapons," Max said. They watched the Netflix TV drama *House of Cards* as an education in American politics. They also took classes in English so that they could better pass as Americans online.

Max and his coworkers read and commented on stories in major US newspapers, including the *New York Times* and the *Washington Post*. They were instructed to insert themselves into the online discussions, to "try to rock the boat." The ultimate goal was to undermine faith in the US political process and the US system of democratic government.

VULNERABLE VOTING MACHINES

Cyberespionage can also involve undermining voting. Hackers can and have targeted databases with lists of registered voters and even voting machines to try to change election results.

Electronic voting machines are vulnerable to hacking, threatening the system of fair elections in the United States and other nations.

For experienced cyberspies, hacking into a voting machine is relatively simple. Even though most voting machines aren't directly connected to the internet, the computers used to program those machines are. It's relatively easy for a cyberspy to inject malicious software into one of these computers to manipulate operations of voting machines.

Even if the voting machines aren't tampered with, cyberspies can affect election results by altering voter registration rolls. They can delete individuals from lists of registered voters; mark legitimate voters as felons, which disqualifies them from voting in many states; or change voters' party affiliations to keep them from voting in party-specific primary elections. Even if only a few thousand votes are suppressed in these ways, it can affect who wins or loses a tight election.

Three years after the 2016 US elections, the US Senate Select Committee on Intelligence released a report revealing that all fifty US states had experienced cyberattacks on their voting systems during the election. These attacks were likely initiated by Russian hackers. The report stated that "Russian cyberactors were in a position to delete or change voter data."

While the Senate report noted that there is no evidence that cyberespionage changed any votes in the 2016 election, continued attacks on the US election system could have significant impact in the future. J. Alex Halderman, a computer science professor at the University of Michigan, says that "it's only a matter of time before some attacker, be it Russia or another hostile country, really does either sabotage or manipulate the country's election infrastructure. . . . Eventually it will happen, unless we take steps to stop it."

How can states protect their voting systems from cyberespionage? The solution is simple: use only paper ballots or require paper backup for electronic voting machines. Paper ballots can't be hacked as can electronic files. As Halderman says, "If you have a paper record that the voter got to inspect, then that can't later be changed by a cyberattack."

VOTING BY MAIL

Starting in the spring of 2020, a virus named SARS-CoV-2, which causes the coronavirus disease 2019 also known as COVID-19, spread around the world, sickening millions and killing hundreds of thousands. Infection spread through close physical contact, so communities made major changes, such as shutting down businesses, to keep people from contracting the disease.

People worried about the virus spreading at polling places, where voters stand in line, interact with poll workers, and touch voting machines and paper ballots. All this activity could help the virus spread from person to person. To help voters avoid infection, many states embraced voting by mail. Certain voters, such as the elderly, have had the option of voting by mail for many years. But after COVID-19 hit, many states changed their election rules to allow more people to vote by mail and stay away from polling places.

Some politicians have resisted the move to mail-in voting. They say that people who are not eligible to vote, such as non–US citizens, will mail in fraudulent ballots. But election officials say there is no evidence that voting by mail results in fraud. Mail-in systems include built-in safeguards, such as matching signatures to prove voter identity and tracking ballots as they travel through the mail. In fact, voting by mail is more secure than voting at electronic voting machines, which are vulnerable to hacking.

CHAPTER 5

CYBERPROPAGANDA:
SPREADING FAKE NEWS

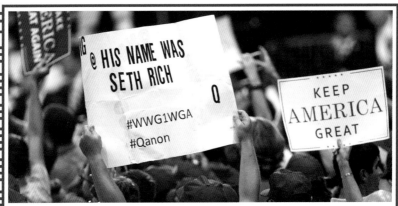

Using hashtags such as #QAnon, many people share and spread propaganda, conspiracy theories, and fake news.

S eth Rich was a twenty-seven-year-old employee of the Democratic National Committee. Born in Omaha, Nebraska, Rich went to college at nearby Creighton University, where he graduated with a degree in political science. After college he left for Washington, DC, and got a job with the DNC.

Rich's friends said he was outgoing and fun-loving but also passionate about protecting and expanding voting rights. He wasn't a high-level staffer or a Washington insider. He was just a guy who loved politics and enjoyed his job.

In the early morning hours of July 10, 2016, Rich was walking home after gathering with friends at Lou's City Bar, a watering hole popular with political staffers. He was talking to his girlfriend on his cell phone about a block and a half from his home when two men accosted him. Rich fought back but unsuccessfully. Police found him with bruises on his face, hands, and knees and two gunshot wounds in his back. Seth Rich died at the scene.

Police investigating the murder concluded that it was a robbery attempt gone wrong. Seven armed robberies had occurred in the same neighborhood in the previous six weeks, and this seemed like yet another.

Rich's murder devastated his family and friends. And if the story had ended there, it would have been tragic enough. But within days, the murder became the focus of a propaganda operation that rocked the 2016 US presidential campaign.

Despite all evidence to the contrary, some people charged that the DNC staffer was the victim of an assassination squad hired by Democratic presidential candidate Hillary Clinton. This false rumor was created by Russian cyberintelligence operatives and spread in the United States by Republican Party operatives and conservative news outlets.

Three days after the murder, on July 13, members of the SVR, Russia's foreign intelligence service (similar to the CIA), wrote and circulated a phony bulletin designed to look like a real US intelligence report. This bulletin stated that Seth Rich, in reality a relatively low-level staffer for the DNC, was on his way to talk to the FBI about corruption in the Clinton campaign when he was murdered by a hit squad hired by the candidate. None of this was true.

Over the next few weeks, the fake story spread to various right-wing (conservative) US websites. The story soon grew to include additional fictitious details, including that Rich, not Russian operatives, had leaked stolen DNC emails to the WikiLeaks organization. Some sites linked Rich's murder to an ongoing FBI investigation of the Clinton Foundation, a nonprofit organization founded by former US president Bill Clinton, Hillary's Clinton's husband.

The RT and Sputnik news organizations, both owned by the Russian government, spread the false story on international and US television. Online, the propaganda spread via Facebook, Twitter, and other social media. Meanwhile, the IRA in Russia created hundreds of fake social media accounts designed to look like those from US political groups and private citizens. These accounts posted or reposted stories about Rich's murder more than two thousand times before the 2016 election. In turn, those posts were reposted by hundreds of thousands of legitimate users who bought into the fiction.

The fake story was ultimately picked up, repeated, and elaborated on by numerous right-wing US radio and television commentators, such as Sean Hannity and Rush Limbaugh. They helped to keep the fiction alive and part of the public conversation during the November election.

After Trump won the presidency, his aides also pushed the story. Steve Bannon, then Trump's chief strategist, texted to a CBS producer that Rich's murder was a "Huge story . . . it was a contract [arranged and paid for] kill, obviously."

Roger Stone, a longtime Trump ally, tweeted a picture of Rich with the message, "another dead body in Clinton's wake . . . Coincidence? I think not."

Why did Russia spread this fictitious narrative about Rich's death? One immediate goal was to promote Trump's candidacy

Fox News host Sean Hannity promoted the fake story linking Seth Rich's murder to the Democratic National Committee.

by pushing the false notion that Clinton was crooked and involved with sinister dealings. After the election, however, the disinformation campaign had a further goal of redirecting attention from Russian's involvement in the 2016 US election. By then the US Department of Justice was investigating Russian election interference, including the hacking of DNC computers and the possible coordination between Trump's campaign and the Russian government.

Deborah Sines was the former assistant US attorney in charge of investigating Rich's case. "It appeared to me that it was a very clear campaign to deflect an ongoing federal criminal investigation. So then you have to look at why is Russia doing this? . . . It's not rocket science before you add it up and you go, 'Oh, if Seth is the leaker to WikiLeaks—it doesn't have anything to do with the Russians.' So of course Russia's interest in doing this is incredibly transparent." The goal was simple, she said. "Let's blame it on Seth Rich. He's a very convenient target."

FAKE OUT

The Seth Rich story is a prime example of fake news. Spread via social media and deliberately deceptive websites, fake news consists of false news stories designed to mislead and misinform. Fake news takes these forms:

- Fictitious news articles, social media posts, and memes. This truly fake news consists of deliberately fabricated items designed to confuse or deceive the public. These items typically consist of misrepresented or totally false "facts" about a topic or person and are often written to resemble legitimate news items. They are sometimes initially posted on websites designed to look like traditional news websites, thus adding the appearance of respectability and trustworthiness.

- Biased or misleading reporting. Although many news outlets strive to be unbiased in their reporting, bias usually creeps in. And some TV networks, publications, and websites lean decidedly to the left (progressive) or right (conservative) of the political spectrum and produce stories designed to advance that perspective. The operators of these biased sources might try to influence people by refusing to cover stories that don't match their viewpoints, by selectively excluding facts that contradict their positions, or by offering reporting slanted in a particular direction. This type of news may not technically be "fake," but it is biased and often misleading.

- Opinion disguised as fact. Many news outlets intermix traditional reporting with personal opinion. This is particularly prevalent on cable news and talk radio stations. The stations don't hire teams of reporters to investigate the truth behind issues and events. Instead, they hire political pundits, who simply give their own opinions rather than reporting the facts. With so many "talking heads" spouting their views, it can be difficult for audiences to know where the real news stops and the opinions begin.

- Conspiracy theories. A conspiracy theory is the mistaken belief that an event is the result of some secret plot, typically carried out by a government, military, or other powerful entity. For example, some Americans believe the conspiracy theory that the US government faked the 1969 moon landing, creating the entire event in a movie studio. (That's not what happened, of course. NASA actually did land astronauts on the moon that year and several times afterward.)

WHEN "FAKE NEWS" ISN'T FAKE

Some politicians have used the term *fake news* to describe legitimate news stories they do not like. Trump is a chief offender. He often dismisses stories that present him in an unfavorable light as "fake news" and calls news sources that oppose him the "fake news media."

The "fake news" targeted by Trump and other politicians isn't really fake—it's real news presented by legitimate news outlets. The politicians call it fake to refute or draw attention away from unflattering facts. However, no one can make a genuine piece of news untrue just by calling it fake. Smearing the source doesn't change the facts.

Still, calling a legitimate story fake can be an effective tool for politicians and other people in power. Questioning the truth of a news item can deflect attention from the facts and denigrate those who report them. The cry of fake news also deliberately misleads the public, causing confusion, mistrust, and divisiveness.

All these forms of fake news have become rampant in the early years of the twenty-first century. Much fake news is of a political nature, designed to inflame passions on one side or another of the political debate. Some fake news does concern nonpolitical topics, however. For example, fake health stories often promise miracle cures for cancer and other deadly diseases.

FAKE NEWS FOR PROFIT

Why do individuals and companies create fake news? Some do it for money, specifically the advertising revenue that a popular website can generate. Online advertising businesses, such as Google AdSense, match advertisers with host websites. When a visitor to a host website clicks an ad on that site, the advertiser pays the website a small fee—typically a fraction of a penny. This is called pay-per-click advertising. The more visitors a site attracts, the more clicks are likely to result. If thousands and thousands of visitors visit the site and click on ads, the pennies start to add up to dollars—sometimes thousands and thousands of dollars.

During the run-up to the 2016 presidential election, some website creators found that fake news stories were extremely popular with visitors—and the more outlandish the stories, the more visitors they got and the more money they made in pay-per-click advertising. In one instance, a group of teenagers and young adults in the small nation of Macedonia created hundreds of fake new websites. These webmasters did not originally have a political agenda but quickly realized that stories with a pro–Donald Trump or anti–Hillary Clinton bias generated the most web traffic and the most revenue. Stories that were completely false but were pro-Trump or anti-Clinton did even better. The owner of one such site averaged more than one million page views per month during the election. Some websites generated more than $10,000 in revenue during that time.

POLITICAL FAKE NEWS

Some fake news is relatively harmless. Other fake news is deliberately designed to spread lies and stir discontent. Cyberpropaganda, or online propaganda, falls into this latter category, as it almost always is part of a larger strategy to achieve a political goal.

Many of those who spread cyberpropaganda are trying to influence public opinion and people's votes. These perpetrators can be political parties or operatives, or foreign governments with a vested interest in another country's election. Russia is one of the largest sources of cyberpropaganda, but it's not the only country engaging in such operations. According to Lee Foster, head of the intelligence team at FireEye Threat Intelligence, a cybersecurity firm, "Multiple foreign actors have demonstrated an ability and willingness to leverage these kinds of influence operations [fake news] in pursuit of their geopolitical goals." Besides Russia, countries working to influence politics in other nations include the United States, China,

Iran, Israel, Saudi Arabia, the United Arab Emirates, and Venezuela. Other countries, including Egypt, Mexico, the Philippines, Qatar, and Turkey, use cyberpropaganda primarily to influence their own internal politics.

Where Russia's cyberpropaganda has tended to support Trump and other right-wing US politicians, other countries have their own political goals. Saudi Arabia, for example, focuses on pressuring other Middle Eastern nations to support it in its rivalry with neighboring nation Qatar. Iran tends to use cyberpropaganda to oppose Trump and his anti-Iranian policies.

As an example of this propaganda, on March 16, 2019, a woman named Alicia Hernan tweeted this about Trump: "That stupid moron doesn't get that . . . by creating bad guys, spewing hate filled words and creating fear of 'others,' his message is spreading to fanatics around the world. Or maybe he does." According to her Twitter profile, Hernan was a wife, mother of two sons, and "lover of peace" who lived in New York. The problem is, Alicia Hernan doesn't exist. The @AliciaHernan3 Twitter account—complete with a picture of a blonde woman wearing large, round-framed glasses—was created by cyberspies in Iran to influence US voters and officials. It was one of more than seven

The Russian government, headquartered at a building called the Kremlin in Moscow, was responsible for creating much of the fake news that disrupted the 2016 US presidential election.

thousand fake accounts that Twitter identified and shut down in 2019. These accounts were part of a concerted effort by Iranian agents to influence public opinion against Trump and in favor of Iran.

HOW CYBERPROPAGANDA SPREADS ONLINE

Cyberpropaganda doesn't just pop up on your social media feed out of nowhere. Most fake news is carefully planned and written for maximum effect.

A fake story is typically part of a larger disinformation campaign, designed to push a particular falsehood, such as the Seth Rich conspiracy theory. The item may originate on a fake news article or might be planted on Facebook, Instagram, Twitter, or another social network. The item typically is posted hundreds or thousands of times by different accounts, most of them representing made-up individuals and many of them operated by bots.

The more an item is posted, the more likely it is to appear in others' social media news feeds. In essence, the fake news takes on a life of its own as the network of fake users spreads the item across social media. The fake news story then starts showing in the news feeds of real users. As people read the fake posts, some will repost them to their own networks of social media contacts. These unwitting users believe the lie or agree with the general sentiment, and seek to share it with their friends and associates. In this way the fake story seeps into the general population, which continues to repost it to friends and followers. If a story goes viral in this way, it will probably jump from social media into traditional media, parroted by pundits on talk radio and cable news, and written about in the opinion pages of local and national newspapers.

The US-based cybersecurity firm Symantec reported on how Russia used Twitter to spread cyberpropaganda during the 2016 elections. The Russian IRA planned and executed the operation, which started with a series of Russia-owned blogs. The IRA posted a variety of fake news stories to these blogs, aimed at both conservative and liberal US voters, and then created 3,836 Twitter accounts to spread that fake news across Twitter. Most of these accounts were operated by bots.

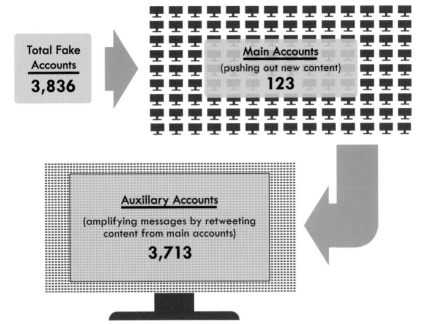

FAKE IRA TWITTER ACCOUNTS, 2016

Total Fake Accounts
3,836

Main Accounts
(pushing out new content)
123

Auxillary Accounts
(amplifying messages by retweeting content from main accounts)
3,713

Before the 2016 US presidential election, Russia's Internet Research Agency used 123 Twitter accounts to create false content. More than 3,700 other accounts spread the fake news by retweeting it.

Usually the bots reposted the original material exactly, although some posts were manually rewritten to slightly change the content. This was an attempt to make the reposts look more authentic and to make it more difficult for Twitter administrators to detect the fakes.

Because people are more apt to retweet posts from others who are following them, the bot accounts signed on to follow 3.2 million legitimate accounts. In turn, the bogus accounts themselves garnered close to 6.4 million followers.

The fake Russian accounts made more than ten million tweets. Many of these tweets were retweeted by politicians and celebrities with large numbers of Twitter followers, including Trump, singer Nicki Minaj, and comedian Sarah Silverman. Even some legitimate news outlets, such as the *Washington Post*, were fooled into retweeting the fake tweets.

WHY (SOME) PEOPLE BELIEVE FAKE NEWS

It may seem odd that so many people believe stories and social media posts that are obviously false. What makes some people believe fake news?

One factor is that people tend to trust others who are like them, in terms of age, gender, or ethnicity. Older white men tend to trust other older white men, for example, and might not trust, say, younger black women. If fake news comes from someone in your own ethnic or political group, you'll be more likely to believe it than a story coming from someone outside that group.

People also tend to believe stories that confirm their preexisting biases and beliefs. This is called confirmation bias. If you believe that Politician A is dishonest and then read a story that says Politician A stole hundreds of thousands of dollars from a charity, you'll be likely to believe that story— even if it's false—because it confirms the bias you already have against Politician A.

A third factor is the continuing "echo chamber" enabled by the internet and hundreds of narrowly focused cable news channels. In this era of news shows targeted to either the left wing or right wing of the general public and personalized social media feeds, it is easy to tune in to only those stories we want to hear. Most people are not exposed to a true range of opinion. The news they do get reinforces their existing opinions. And the more a person hears the same thing over and over, the more likely the person will believe it, whether it's true or not. As psychologist Lisa Fazio of Vanderbilt University in Tennessee explains, the more you hear something, the more "you'll have this gut-level feeling that maybe it's true."

THE VERY REAL DANGERS OF FAKE NEWS

According to the US think tank the Pew Research Center, half of all Americans view fake news as a bigger threat to US society than violent crime, climate change, racism, illegal immigration, or terrorism. More than two-thirds say that the confusion created by fake news has greatly affected their confidence in government, and half say it's affected their confidence in one another. People don't know whom or what sources to trust anymore.

Fake news even undermines the foundations of our democratic society. Voters need factual information to make informed choices during elections, but fake news makes it difficult to separate fact and fiction. Citizens also need factual information about their government, and fake news disrupts this flow of information. Amy Mitchell, the Pew Research Center's director of journalism research, says, "The impact of made-up news goes beyond exposure to it and confusion about what is factual. Americans see it influencing the core functions of our democratic system."

Cyberpropaganda from political extremists or foreign countries threatens to upend not just public trust in the election process but the elections themselves. Disinformation campaigns, even when proven false, can sway voters away from or toward a certain candidate. And even just a few thousand voters affected by fake news stories can swing a close election from one candidate to another.

Fake news and cyberpropaganda are having a very real impact on our society. It's not difficult to imagine one nation going to war with another based on fabricated information. With today's social media tools, it's easier than ever to influence individuals and even entire nations.

CHAPTER 6

CYBERATTACKS:
RANSOMWARE AND MORE

A ransomware attack crippled operations at Hollywood Presbyterian Medical Center in 2016.

Hollywood Presbyterian Medical Center (HPMC), in Los Angeles, California, has more than 424 beds. More than five hundred doctors treat more than sixteen thousand patients a year there.

On February 5, 2016, an employee using a hospital computer opened an email message that appeared to have an attached

Microsoft Word document containing an invoice. The employee clicked to open the attachment, but it wasn't a Word document. The attachment was actually a malicious file that contained the Locky computer virus. Locky is ransomware, designed to lock users out of infected computers unless they pay money.

The Locky virus infected the employee's computer and quickly spread throughout the hospital's network of computers. Almost immediately, staff throughout the hospital reported that they were unable to access the hospital's network.

The hospital immediately declared a state of emergency. To keep the virus from spreading further, the entire computer system was taken off-line. Doctors were unable to access patients' medical histories. They couldn't share the results of CT scans, X-rays, and other medical tests. The hospital's pharmacy was shut down.

At the front desk, patient admission systems were in chaos. Staff resorted to using pen and paper to sign in new patients. Patients scheduled for elective, or optional, medical procedures were sent home and told to reschedule. Some patients were sent to other hospitals.

The hospital soon received a digital ransom notice, splashed across the screens of all the infected computers. It read as follows:

!!! IMPORTANT INFORMATION !!!!
All of your files are encrypted with the RSA-2048 and AES-128 ciphers . . .
Decrypting of your files is only possible with the private key and decrypt program, which is on our secret server.

The rest of the message instructed the hospital to click a link to receive the key that would enable restoration of its files. When hospital IT staff clicked the link, they received instructions on how to pay a ransom of 40 Bitcoin, a type of digital currency. With Bitcoin transactions, the identities of users can be kept secret, which makes payments difficult to track and criminal Bitcoin users hard to find.

The hospital did not have backup data and had no choice but to pay the ransom. HPMC president Allen Stefanek issued a notice that stated, "The quickest and most efficient way to restore our systems and administrative functions was to pay the ransom. In the best interest of restoring normal operations, we did this."

It took HPMC officials several days to arrange the purchase of 40 Bitcoin, then worth about $17,000 (the value of Bitcoin changes daily, just like shares of stock), and to transfer the funds to the attacker's online bank account. Ten days after the attack, on February 15, the extortionists unlocked the computers and the hospital was able to resume all services.

The Los Angeles Police Department and the FBI investigated the crime but were unable to identify the perpetrators. HPMC reported no further attacks, but other cyberextortionists saw an opportunity to make money by imitating the attack. Cybersecurity firm Symantec reported that within a week of the HPMC payment, its security software detected and destroyed nearly five million emails containing the Locky virus.

CYBERATTACKS FOR PROFIT

A ransomware attack is extortion initiated over the internet—a cyberattack for profit. Since earlier times, criminals have kidnapped individuals and held them captive until their family members or others paid a ransom. In the modern era, the cyberextortionist holds the victim's computers and data hostage and won't release them until a ransom is paid.

Some cyberextortionists focus on a single business or government entity. Others send ransomware to a large number of targets, assuming that at least a few recipients will click on a link and release the virus onto their computers.

BITCOIN

Most cyberextortionists demand payment in Bitcoin, a type of cryptocurrency. Cryptocurrency is not a physical currency made up of bills and coins. A cryptocurrency such as Bitcoin is just an encrypted computer file. Bitcoin is based on open-source code, so it has no controlling entity, such as a central bank. It is distributed online via peer-to-peer file-trading networks.

People who make and receive payments in Bitcoin can keep their identities secret. This makes Bitcoin transactions hard to trace. It also makes the currency ideal for criminal transactions, such as drug deals and payments to cyberextortionists, who naturally want to evade law enforcement.

Bitcoin is traded on stock exchanges much like shares in companies, so its value fluctuates daily. As of May 2020, a single Bitcoin was worth about $8,850 US dollars—although it traded for as high as $12,000 and as low as $3,000 during the previous year.

A ransomware attack can be triggered in one of several ways. The first and most common is via a phishing email. When an unsuspecting victim clicks a link in the email and enters their username and password, the attacker gets access to the system and can plant the ransomware. Another common approach is to send the victim an email with an ordinary-looking attachment. When the user opens the attachment, the ransomware infects the host system.

Some cyberextortionists launch their attacks immediately on the initial infection. Others wait patiently for the ransomware to spread across large computer systems. Some ransomware attacks happen weeks or months after initial infections.

Once the extortionist initiates the attack, the ransomware goes to work. The malicious software encrypts (encodes) data across the infected system so that authorized users can't access it. Some ransomware also encrypts the operating system of the infected computers, making the computers useless. The most sophisticated ransomware is also able to infect data backups, so the targeted organization can't restore data from a previous date. Users at the targeted entity are frozen out of the entire computer system.

Cyberextortionists, who have carefully covered their tracks online, then send victims a ransom notice. This notice may automatically appear on the screens of infected computers, or it may arrive in an email message. The message notifies victims that their computers and data are encrypted and provides information on how to satisfy attackers' demands. This typically involves making a payment, usually in Bitcoin, to an untraceable online bank account. Ransom demands can range from several thousand dollars to several million. Then victims can either pay the ransom or not.

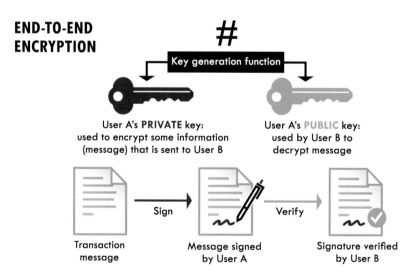

END-TO-END ENCRYPTION

Key generation function

User A's **PRIVATE** key: used to encrypt some information (message) that is sent to User B

User A's **PUBLIC** key: used by User B to decrypt message

Transaction message

Sign

Message signed by User A

Verify

Signature verified by User B

A system called end-to-end encryption helps keep digital messages safe from intruders. The sender and recipient use keys to encrypt and decrypt information. A signature verification step ensures that an intruder doesn't impersonate the recipient and intercept the message.

If a company or organization chooses not to pay the ransom, it can attempt to restore affected data from a previous data backup. This may be effective, depending on whether the ransomware has also frozen the backup. If the entire computer system is locked up, the organization may need to purchase new computers and servers. The cost to proceed without paying the ransom may exceed the price of the ransom.

Paying the ransom as demanded carries its own risks. The cyberextortionist may take the money and run, leaving the infected systems inoperable. Even if the cyberextortionist provides the key to decrypt the locked data, the victim might still encounter problems. Not all affected data is always recoverable, and some damage to files or systems may be irreparable. The targeted entity loses the money it costs to be off-line for days or weeks—and the time and expense of bringing affected systems back online.

The City of Baltimore, Maryland, was the target of a ransomware attack in May 2019. The cyberextortionists demanded a ransom of $76,000, but Mayor Bernard C. Young and city officials refused to give in to the demand. Instead, the city spent many times more than that—about $10 million—to fix its damaged computer systems and restore data.

In contrast, the City of Riviera Beach, Florida, responded to a similar ransomware attack the same month by agreeing to pay the ransom. Attackers demanded a payment of 65 Bitcoin, then worth about $592,000. Once it was paid, the attackers provided the appropriate decryption key, and the city had 90 percent of its data back and systems up and running again within sixty days.

THE REAL COST OF CYBEREXTORTION

Ransomware attacks are on the rise. "Ransomware is a big problem that is continuing to grow," says Allan Liska, senior solutions architect with Recorded Future, a cybersecurity company. "It is also a big money-making opportunity for both experienced and new cybercriminals. Which means the bad guys are devoting a lot of resources to developing new methods to deliver ransomware."

According to a report from cybersecurity firm Emsisoft, 948 government agencies, schools, and health-care businesses in the United States were hit by ransomware attacks in 2019. The targets included 759 hospitals and health-care providers, 103 state and local

THE FBI SAYS, DON'T DEAL WITH CRIMINALS

While many companies and institutions are willing to pay the ransom to get their systems back up and running quickly after a ransomware attack, the FBI and other law enforcement officials discourage giving in to attackers' demands. They say that giving the attackers what they want only encourages further criminal activity.

As with human kidnapping cases, there's no guarantee that if a victim pays the ransom, the attackers will release the data being held hostage. And even if the affected files are decrypted, they may have gotten corrupted during the ransomware attack and become useless.

The FBI also warns that ransomware might not be the only threat to a victim's computer system. Hackers might insert other kinds of malware along with the ransomware, and even if the victim pays the ransom, that malware can remain and do damage. So the FBI recommends that instead of paying a hacker's ransom, victims perform a full fix of any infected systems, including wiping (deleting all data from) their computers and restoring data from off-line backups.

Victims also face the nightmare scenario of a second cyberextortion attack. The same attackers might attack again, or other criminals might view the victim as an easy target and launch their own attacks. So cybersecurity experts encourage companies and organizations that are ransomware attack victims to strengthen security systems to guard against future attacks.

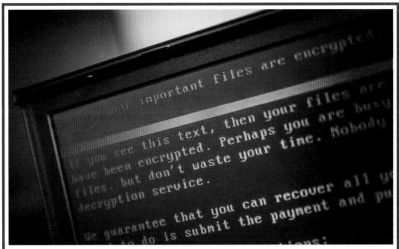

During a 2017 attack, cyberextortionists targeted Britain's National Health Service and many other organizations around the world. This laptop computer shows the ransom message.

governments, and eighty-six colleges, universities, and school districts. The cost of these attacks was estimated to be as high as $7.5 billion. That includes ransom payments, the restoration of backed-up data, the purchase of replacement equipment, and lost business income during downtime.

Aside from the financial costs, the attacks had untold other impacts. During attacks on hospitals, admissions were halted and emergency patients often had to be sent to other sites. Tests and surgical procedures were postponed or canceled. Doctors couldn't access patient records, and hospitals couldn't send bills or accept payments.

During attacks on cities and government agencies, 911 services were interrupted. Emergency dispatchers, without access to computers, had to rely on printed maps and paper logs. Police were unable to access details about individuals' criminal histories or those who were wanted for arrest. Building access and security systems stopped working, and jail doors couldn't be remotely opened. Utility bills couldn't be sent, and customer payments couldn't be accepted. Property sales were put on hold, and driver's licenses couldn't be issued or renewed. Some email and phone systems stopped working, and websites went off-line.

Educational institutions and school districts were also hit hard. Records of students' grades were lost, and schools couldn't access students' medical records. Some schools were forced to close.

It could have been worse. The damage to hospital and government computer systems could have resulted in the death of patients, crime victims, or public workers. Fabian Wosar, chief technical officer of Emsisoft, said, "The fact that there were no confirmed ransomware-related deaths in 2019 is simply due to good luck, and that luck may not continue into 2020."

WHO ARE THE CYBEREXTORTIONISTS?

Who is to blame for ransomware attacks? Even though the perpetrators try hard to cover their digital tracks, including demanding payment in untraceable cybercurrency, officials can trace most attacks to two types of suspects.

The first are organized criminal groups, many operating out of eastern Europe. These criminal organizations are in it for the money. They employ teams of professional hackers to develop ransomware, exploit vulnerabilities in targeted networks, handle ransom payments, and hide collected funds. Ransomware attacks on the computer servers of the State of Louisiana and the City of New Orleans in 2019 are believed to be the work of eastern European crime organizations. "It's a criminal organization running this thing," said Wesley McGrew, director of cyberoperations at the cybersecurity firm Horne Cyber.

The other perpetrators are national governments. Most state-led cyberextortion schemes come from countries suffering from heavy global sanctions. These economic actions are taken to persuade nations to change their policies. For example, the United States has refused to trade or do business with Iran because it says Iran is trying to create deadly nuclear weapons. Many nations have imposed sanctions on Russia because of its aggression toward neighboring nations. Because of sanctions, Iran, North Korea, and Russia are short on funds. As with organized crime groups, they sometimes use ransomware attacks to raise money. Some of the biggest ransomware attacks have been traced to state-sponsored groups. These include the following:

- NotPetya. This 2017 attack targeted businesses in Ukraine and across Europe. It was traced to GRU, the Russian military's official spy agency.
- WannaCry. This attack, also in 2017, affected more than two hundred thousand businesses in 150 countries. It was blamed on Lazarus, a cybercriminal group linked to the North Korean government.
- SamSam. These 2018 attacks targeted more than two hundred US and Canadian cities and caused more than $30 million in damages. The DOJ charged two Iranian men with orchestrating these attacks. Justice Department officials believe the men acted with the permission of the Iranian government.

It appears that few ransomware attacks involve individual hackers. The attacks are typically too complex to be managed by a single person, requiring the larger operations of organized crime or governments.

ANATOMY OF A CYBERATTACK

There is no typical cyberattack. Each attack is different, and even the same cybercriminals often use different techniques from one attack to the next. While ransomware is used for financial gain, cyberattackers can use other types of malware to steal or destroy data, spread disinformation, or disable victims' computers, networks, and any technology connected to those networks.

Even though the malware might be different, many cyberattacks are similar. Attackers learn from their mistakes, refine their techniques, and develop new and more effective malware.

ZOMBIES ATTACK!

Many widespread cyberattacks, especially distributed denial-of-service (DDoS) attacks, are conducted by vast armies of hijacked computers. These are computers infected with malware that lets a third party control them without the owners' permission. The hijacked computers become "zombies" controlled by the attacker. A group of these hijacked computers is called a botnet. Besides computers, a botnet might include smart devices connected to the internet, such as smartphones, smart speakers, and smart light bulbs. Most owners of zombie devices have no idea that their machines have been infected, hijacked, and used in cyberattacks.

Many cyberattacks start with reconnaissance. The attacker studies potential targets to determine whom, where, and how to attack. Attackers might weed out targets with strong security systems or those that offer little valuable data. Some attackers are less picky. They simply send out mass phishing messages to stolen email lists and hope that a certain percentage of recipients take the bait.

No matter how the target is identified, the cyberattackers will somehow infiltrate the target computer or computer network. They might use spear phishing to obtain login credentials, find an open backdoor in the system, or exploit a flaw in the software to gain entry to the network.

Once a cyberattacker has penetrated the target system, the actual attack occurs. An attacker might install malware designed to perform some further action, such as encrypting data or taking control of the system. The attacker might root around the system, looking for valuable data to download. Or the attacker might simply destroy data or disable the system.

ATTACK DISTRIBUTION, 2019

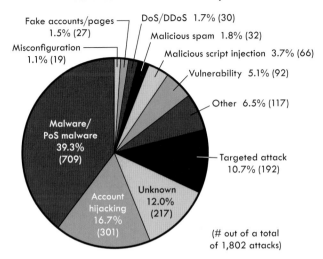

Fake accounts/pages 1.5% (27)

Misconfiguration 1.1% (19)

DoS/DDoS 1.7% (30)

Malicious spam 1.8% (32)

Malicious script injection 3.7% (66)

Vulnerability 5.1% (92)

Other 6.5% (117)

Malware/PoS malware 39.3% (709)

Targeted attack 10.7% (192)

Account hijacking 16.7% (301)

Unknown 12.0% (217)

(# out of a total of 1,802 attacks)

TARGET DISTRIBUTION, 2019

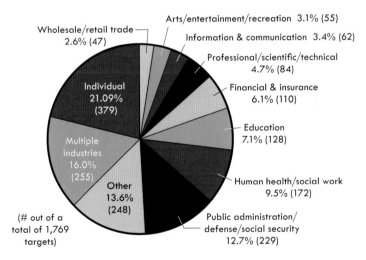

Wholesale/retail trade 2.6% (47)

Arts/entertainment/recreation 3.1% (55)

Information & communication 3.4% (62)

Professional/scientific/technical 4.7% (84)

Individual 21.09% (379)

Financial & insurance 6.1% (110)

Education 7.1% (128)

Multiple industries 16.0% (255)

Human health/social work 9.5% (172)

Other 13.6% (248)

Public administration/defense/social security 12.7% (229)

(# out of a total of 1,769 targets)

Cybercriminals can attack in many different ways and can target any individual, business, or organization with an internet connection. The top pie chart shows that in 2019, malware accounted for the largest percentage of cyberattacks worldwide. Account hijacking was the second most common type of attack in 2019. The bottom pie chart shows that cybercriminals most often targeted individuals in 2019.

THE CYBERARSENAL

Cyberattacks can take a variety of forms. For instance, DDoS attacks are designed to temporarily disable the target system. The attacker generally employs a botnet to send tens of thousands of spam messages or requests to a website or network. The huge number of incoming messages overwhelms the target and forces it off-line.

In a man-in-the-middle (MitM) attack, the attacker intercepts messages between a website or network and a legitimate customer, employee, or other site user. Neither party realizes that an intruder is listening in on their communications. In this type of attack, the intruder can steal a user's login credentials, credit card numbers, and other confidential information. Posing as the user, the intruder can also plant malware, steal data, or send out phishing messages.

Another type of attack exploits vulnerabilities in the Structured Query Language (SQL), a programming language commonly used to manage large databases. In SQL attacks, the attacker injects malicious code into the database server. The infection allows the attacker to access confidential information stored in the database, such as customer or credit card data.

No matter what type of attack the criminal uses, everything is done in the utmost secrecy. Few attackers want to announce their presence in an invaded system or take credit for successful attacks. This would only draw unwanted attention from cybersecurity staff and law enforcement and would hinder any future operations. So the final step in most attacks is sanitation—removing all traces that the attacker was there. This is done by editing or destroying user logs and deleting any files associated with the attack.

THE LARGEST DDOS ATTACK
IN HISTORY (SO FAR)

In February 2020, Amazon Web Services (AWS) was the victim of the single largest DDoS attack on record. AWS is a web hosting service used by big companies such as Netflix, LinkedIn, Facebook, and ESPN. The attack was directed against an unnamed AWS client. It consumed a record 2.3 terabits of bandwidth—five times more than the typical DDoS attack.

AWS's threat protection service, AWS Shield, first detected the attack on February 17. Once activated, AWS Shield was able to block the attack, with no disruption to the targeted servers, so the targeted company suffered no computer downtime. Even so, AWS could not stop the incoming traffic from the cyberattackers, which continued for three days before subsiding.

Cybersecurity experts don't know who initiated the AWS attack or why. Prior to the attack, the largest DDoS attack was recorded two years before, in February 2018. That attack targeted GitHub, an online platform for software developers. The GitHub attack clocked in at 1.35 terabits.

CYBERTERRORISM:
ATTACKING SYSTEMS AND INFRASTRUCTURE

National security experts fear a cyberattack on the US electrical grid. Such an attack would knock out all communications, shut down machinery, and hurt businesses.

Imagine this scenario. It is a typical weekday in the United States. The springtime weather is quite mild. Adults are at work or on their way there. Children are at school. The talking heads on all major cable news networks are discussing something controversial the president said the day before.

Shortly after 10:00 a.m., the big broadcasting networks break into their coverage to report that a major terrorist organization has announced on social media that it intends to shut down part of the country's electrical power grid. The terrorists say they are taking action as vengeance for a US military action in their homeland. The group says the power grid will go off-line at 4:00 p.m. that day and stay off-line for six hours.

At precisely 4:00 p.m. the power goes off across Idaho, Oregon, and Washington. Homes and offices there go dark. Hospitals must revert to emergency generators. Stoplights and streetlights stop working. Television and radio stations go off the air, and cable TV and internet service go down. Life in those three states slows to a standstill.

At 10:00 p.m. the power comes back on, as promised. But that doesn't end the attack.

Two days later, the same terrorist group announces that it will shut down the main telecommunication lines between the eastern and western coasts of the United States for a half day, starting the next day at noon. The group follows through, disrupting all cross-country communications. The day following, the group says it will take down the air traffic control system in and around New York City. That happens too, grounding all air traffic in the region.

Over the next days and weeks, the group makes similar threats, successfully executing them all. The US public demands that the government take action, except officials can't do anything. The country is held hostage by the terrorists, businesses shut down and go broke, and American society descends into chaos.

This particular cyberterrorist attack didn't happen, but something like it could. This scenario was envisioned by a group of fifty prominent computer scientists back in 2002, following the September 11, 2001 (9/11), terrorist attacks on the World Trade Center in New York and the Pentagon near Washington, DC. In a joint letter to then president George W. Bush, the scientists warned, "Our nation is at grave risk of a cyber attack that could devastate the national psyche and economy more broadly than did the September 11th attack. We, as concerned scientists and leaders, seek your help and offer ours. The critical infrastructure of the United States, including electrical power, finance, telecommunications, health care, transportation, water, defense and the internet, is highly vulnerable to cyber attack."

Close to two decades later, the United States is still at risk of this type of devastating cyberterrorist attack. To some experts it isn't a matter of *if* a major cyberterrorist attack will happen. It's only a matter of *when*.

WHAT IS CYBERTERRORISM?

The FBI defines cyberterrorism as any "premeditated, politically motivated attack against information, computer systems, computer programs, and data which results in violence against non-combatant targets by sub-national groups or clandestine agents." Cyberterrorism goes beyond ransomware, data theft, and similar cyberattacks carried out for profit. Instead, cyberterrorists aim to cause large-scale panic or loss of life by attacking critical civilian and government infrastructure, such as power networks, financial systems, hospitals, and emergency services.

Luke Dembosky, former deputy assistant attorney general for national security at the DOJ, said, "[Cyberterrorism] is not the same as the loss of your credit card data in a breach. . . . This is about life and death, and when it comes to providing medical care or not, or being able to access patient records, keeping the power grid on, the trading platform [stock market] going, it becomes a much larger risk area."

TERRORISTS ONLINE

Like all organizations, terrorists use the internet for communications. Terrorist groups use websites to promote their ideologies, enlist supporters, and share information, including instructions for building bombs. Terrorists fill social media with propaganda, such as slick recruitment videos. For example, a 2016 recruitment video from al-Shabaab, al-Qaeda's Somalian affiliate, included a clip of Trump calling for a US ban on immigrants who practice Islam. The video was designed to stir up hatred toward the United States and to recruit anti-American supporters.

Terrorists also use tools freely available over the internet to plan their attacks. They use securely encrypted email and messaging apps, chat rooms, and message forums. For example, the Taliban used the free Google Maps service to plan its 2012 raid on Camp Bastion, a British airbase in Afghanistan.

Cyberterrorists employ many of the same methods as other cyberattackers. A cyberterrorist attack can involve phishing and other social engineering techniques to gain entrance into a targeted system, and then infecting that system with computer viruses and other malware. Some cyberterrorism attacks resemble cyberextortion, disabling data and computer systems with ransomware until a ransom is paid to the terrorists.

Cyberterrorism is appealing to terrorist groups for many reasons. First, compared to conventional terrorist methods, such as bombings and hijackings, cyberterrorism requires fewer financial resources. The only tools needed are computers and an internet connection. Second, cyberattacks are easier to conduct anonymously. In a conventional terrorist attack, law enforcement might identify the terrorists using eyewitness accounts or surveillance camera footage. But in cyberterrorism, the malware that attacks computers often can't be traced to a specific terrorist group. Third, cyberterrorism presents a large number of potential targets and is not limited by geographical boundaries—attackers can operate from anywhere and target anyplace else on Earth via only a computer network. While cyberterrorism does require extensive technological expertise, cyberterrorists can hire experts with the skills they need.

The intent of most terrorist attacks is not necessarily to kill hundreds of people but rather to frighten millions—to throw the public into mass panic. Particularly worrisome to many experts is an attack that could take out the electrical power grid for an entire county or region. Lieutenant General Vincent Stewart, former head of US Cyber Command, warns that if large parts of a country "lose power for an extended period of time, it is not just about the inconvenience of losing power. . . . Think about the impact on hospitals and refrigerated medicines." Without electric power, food would spoil in refrigerators. Gas pumps and ATMs wouldn't work. Systems for pumping water would shut down. In such a scenario, panic would likely ensue.

WHO ARE THE CYBERTERRORISTS?

Cyberterrorists might work for a well-known terrorist organization, such as ISIS, or they might work on behalf of a government. According to the *Worldwide Threat Assessment of the US Intelligence Community*, prepared for the US Senate Select Committee on Intelligence, "China, Russia, Iran, and North Korea increasingly use cyberoperations to threaten both minds and machines in an expanding number of ways." Some governments employ and carry out cyberattacks directly. That is, government agents carry out the attacks. Some cyberterrorists are not officially affiliated with their host countries but act on behalf of those countries to promote national interests. For example, the hacktivist group Pakistan Cyber Army is not an official arm of the Pakistani government, but the group has conducted dozens of cyberterrorist attacks on websites in India, China, and Israel—all countries thought to be hostile to Pakistan.

ISIS AND CYBERTERRORISM

ISIS is one of the most technologically advanced terrorist groups. Traditionally, ISIS used suicide bombings and guerrilla attacks to terrorize its opponents throughout the Middle East. But its strategy is constantly evolving.

In recent years ISIS has developed extensive cyber capability, employing a variety of subgroups within the larger organization. Greek researchers Dominika Giantas and Dimitrios Stergiou have mapped ISIS's cyber organizations, noting each group's responsibilities. For instance, the Kalashnikov E-Security Team exists primarily to provide technical support to ISIS's other cyberterrorism teams. The Islamic State Hacking Division is responsible for infiltrating foreign websites and stealing confidential data.

The ISIS logo appears on a hacked computer screen.

In 2013 the Syrian Electronic Army, a group associated with but not sponsored by the Syrian government, attacked multiple media websites, including the sites of the *New York Times*, the Huffington Post, and Twitter. They all went off-line for several hours. The group considered these media organizations to be hostile to Syrian president Bashar al-Assad. It attacked the media organizations in retaliation for criticizing al-Assad's abuses, including the killing of thousands of Syrian civilians.

Middle East–based terrorist groups such as ISIS, al-Qaeda, and the Taliban are expanding their efforts into cyberspace. These groups once used weapons such as firearms and explosives to carry out their attacks. In the twenty-first century they also employ new methods, such as cyberterrorism. In 2003 former US presidential adviser for cybersecurity Richard Clarke said, "The fact that these people are gathering skills in cyber war capability is very troubling, combined with the fact that we know that they're looking on the web for hacking tools. We know that because we've seized some of their computers. It suggests to me that . . . someday we may see al-Qaeda . . . use cyberspace as a vehicle for attacking infrastructure, not with bombs but with bytes."

The US Department of Homeland Security said in a 2005 report, "We anticipate more substantial cyber threats are possible in the future as a more technically competent generation enters the ranks."

That "technically competent generation" referred to in 2005 has come of age, and terrorist groups of all types are attempting to recruit young people with IT skills. These groups are starting to make their cyber abilities known. For example, in 2015 the Cyber Caliphate Army (CCA), a subgroup of ISIS, hacked into the Twitter

Terrorists don't just use guns and bombs anymore. They also target their enemies using cyberattacks.

and YouTube accounts of US Central Command. The group posted a variety of threats and pro-ISIS messages. One message read, ". . . the CyberCaliphate continues its CyberJihad [cyberwar on behalf of Islam]." Another warned, "American soldiers, we are coming, watch your back." Despite the threats, no physical attacks followed, and Central Command regained control of its hacked accounts within twenty-four hours.

AN ESCALATING THREAT

The US public is certainly fearful of cyberterrorism. A 2018 Gallup poll found that 81 percent of those surveyed viewed cyberterrorism as a critical threat to the country—a bigger threat than traditional terrorist attacks.

The US military is also worried about the threat. According to a 2018 survey by *Military Times*, 89 percent of military personnel surveyed said that cyberterrorism was a significant or very significant threat. The service members said that cyberterrorism was a greater threat than that posed by the traditional military forces of Russia, China, or North Korea.

By the 2020s, the United States had seen fewer actual cyberterrorism attacks than the group of scientists had predicted after 9/11. While websites have been hacked, the United States has seen no large-scale cyberterrorist attack on its essential infrastructure, such as its power grid, oil pipelines, or transportation systems. But it is likely that cyberterrorists in the near future will use all their cybertools, including ransomware, to raise funds, plan, and initiate such attacks.

The internet expands the reach of terrorist networks that have historically been limited geographically. Before the world was digitally connected, terrorist groups usually struck close to home. They didn't have enough money to send attackers to distant nations. But in the digital age, terrorists can strike any target that has an internet connection, anywhere in the world. As Ian Bremmer, president of the Eurasia Group political consulting firm, warns, "When Boko Haram [an ISIS subgroup in West Africa] or ISIS start having [cyber capabilities], the threat to the United States suddenly becomes a hell of a lot greater."

CHAPTER 8

CYBERWARFARE:
NATION VERSUS NATION, ONLINE

If cyberwarfare knocks out power in a major city, society can descend into fear and chaos.

On December 16, 2016, in Kiev, the capital of Ukraine, Oleksii Yasinsky was sitting in his living room watching a movie with his wife and teenage son. At midnight the TV suddenly went dark, along with all the lights in their apartment. Yasinsky went into the kitchen to get some candles.

While he was lighting the candles, Yasinsky looked out his kitchen window. The city beyond was totally dark. There wasn't a single light on in any of the high-rise apartment buildings and condos across the street. The power was out across the entire city.

Lights, TVs, internet connections, and heating systems all shut down without power. The temperature outside was near 0°F (−18°C) and falling. Yasinsky knew that it wouldn't take long before water pipes in buildings started to freeze. He thought about breaking out blankets and coats for when the temperature started to drop inside his apartment.

Fortunately for Yasinsky and the other residents of Kiev, the power outage lasted just an hour. But the threat that it represented was much greater. The power had gone out in Kiev because of a Russian cyberattack.

Ukraine is in northern Europe, bordering Russia. It was formerly a part of the Union of Soviet Socialist Republics (USSR), also known as the Soviet Union. When the Soviet Union dissolved in 1991, Ukraine became an independent nation.

Russia was the biggest and most powerful republic in the Soviet Union. After the Soviet Union split apart, Russia wanted to maintain its dominance in northern Europe. It viewed the Crimean Peninsula, on Ukraine's side of the Russian-Ukrainian border and jutting into the Black Sea, as essential to its strategic position in the region. Russia was able to keep a naval fleet stationed in Crimea after the fall of the Soviet Union, thanks to the Kharkiv Pact, a treaty it signed with Ukraine. The treaty was unpopular with many

Ukrainians. They did not want the Russian navy stationed within their borders.

In early 2014, Ukraine began strengthening ties with the democratic nations of western Europe. Russia felt that Ukraine's shifting alliances threatened its agreement regarding Crimea. Worried that its fleet would be ousted from Crimea, Russia quickly moved special forces troops into the peninsula, effectively invading Ukraine.

Russia's physical invasion of Ukraine was accompanied by cyberattacks. Three days before Ukraine's presidential election in May 2014, Russia attacked Ukraine's Central Election Commission, disabling parts of its computer network. This was followed by a number of wiper malware attacks, which destroyed operating systems, data, and backup data on hundreds of infected machines. The attack hit the airport in Kiev and the railway system, grounding planes and shutting down rail travel.

The cyberattacks continued throughout 2014 and 2015. The day before Christmas in 2015, Russia launched a devastating attack on three Ukrainian regional utility companies. This created the first known blackout to be caused by a cyberattack. More than 225,000 citizens lost power for six hours.

More Russian cyberattacks followed in 2016, hitting Ukraine's treasury, ministry of defense, power systems, and transportation networks. The cyberattack on Kiev's power grid that affected Oleksii Yasinsky and his family was part of the assault. "The main goal is to destabilize Ukraine . . . to make chaos," said Valentyn Nalyvaichenko, former head of the Security Service of Ukraine.

The cyberattacks continued into 2017, when Russian cyberspies hacked into a Ukrainian accounting firm to launch NotPetya malware. This automated computer worm spread almost instantly to 10 percent of the computers in the country and permanently deleted data on infected computers. NotPetya halted the operations of cash registers and credit card systems, ATMs, banks, hospitals, and other critical infrastructure across Ukraine. The malware also spread across Ukraine's borders to hit computers throughout Europe and in the United States, causing an estimated $10 billion in damage.

Some believe that World War III, if and when it comes, won't involve bombs, troops, or submarines. Instead, it will be a cyberwar, such as the one Russia continues to wage against Ukraine, fought by hackers typing on keyboards. It may sound like a fantasy, but it's a possibility—and the United States and other nations may be ill-equipped to defend against it.

CYBERWARFARE: IT'S NOT FICTION ANYMORE

Cybersecurity experts define cyberwar as the use of digital technology to attack a nation, causing damage that can be just as devastating as that inflicted during conventional warfare. Cyberwar involves attacks on computers and the systems they run, from power plants and health-care systems to missile defense systems. The scenarios are not fictional. Small cyberwars have already begun.

RUSSIA VERSUS ESTONIA

One of the first instances of cyberwarfare between two nations occurred in Estonia in 2007. Estonia is a former Soviet republic, as Ukraine is. And like Ukraine, it is still somewhat under the influence of neighboring Russia.

In the spring of 2007, the government of Estonia decided to move a Soviet-era statue of a Russian soldier from its place in the center of Tallinn, the country's capital. This move disturbed the nation's Russian-speaking minority and led to a series of DDoS attacks on more than one hundred Estonian banking, media, and government websites.

The cyberattacks, which continued for weeks, came from a network of hijacked computers around the world. They had been infected with malware and were controlled by groups within neighboring Russia. Security experts believe the Russian government either condoned or directly authorized the attacks.

RUSSIA VERSUS GEORGIA

The following year, during the summer of 2008, similar cyberattacks hit the nation of Georgia, another former Soviet republic that borders Russia. These attacks struck more than one-third of Georgia's websites and were timed to accompany Russia's physical invasion of Georgia.

The Russian invasion was staged to support pro-Russian ethnic groups in Georgia. During the attack, Russian tanks rolled into the Georgian capital of Tbilisi and the Russian naval fleet blockaded the country's coastline on the Black Sea. This made the 2008 Russo-Georgian War the first hybrid conventional and cyberwar in history.

During war with Georgia in 2008, Russia first attacked Georgian websites, crippling the nation's businesses, government, and communications. Then the Russian army invaded with tanks and teams of soldiers.

NORTH KOREA VERSUS SOUTH KOREA

Russia isn't the only state actor engaging in cyberwarfare with its enemies. North Korea has conducted multiple cyberattacks against neighboring South Korea through an elite hacking unit known as Bureau 121. This unit is staffed with the best computer science students from the country's Hamheung Computer Technology University, trained in the latest computing, networking, and data processing technologies.

North Korea has launched cyberattacks on a major South Korean bank, three South Korean media outlets, and a South Korean power company. Cyberexperts think that Bureau 121 was also part of North Korea's 2014 cyberattack on Sony Pictures in the United States.

The United States has also engaged in cyberwarfare. One well-known incident involved efforts to halt Iran's growing nuclear weapons program.

In 2009 Iran was moving aggressively to develop deadly nuclear weapons. The United States wanted to shut down this program, which was seen as a threat to peace in the Middle East. The United States could have destroyed Iran's nuclear facilities with bombs, but such an attack might have led to a prolonged war between the two nations. Desiring a different solution, the United States turned to its cyberintelligence operations.

Working with computer experts in Israel, an ally of the United States, cyberspies in the NSA developed a strain of malware known as Stuxnet. This computer worm was loaded onto a USB drive. Although the details of the attack are secret, a spy used the drive to infect computers at fifteen Iranian government and industrial facilities. One of the sites was Iran's nuclear production facility in Natanz.

Workers unload nuclear fuel at a power plant in Iran. Worried that Iran would use its nuclear facilities to develop weapons, the United States launched a malware attack on Iranian nuclear equipment in 2009.

The Stuxnet virus was designed to destroy the 6.5-foot-tall (2 m) aluminum centrifuges that Iran used to enrich uranium to make nuclear fuel. It worked by injecting malicious commands into the centrifuge controllers. These commands sped up the centrifuges until they literally tore themselves apart. Stuxnet was successful, destroying more than one thousand centrifuges.

Iran has mounted attacks of its own against the United States and its allies. In August 2012, for instance, Iran attacked computers of Saudi Aramco, an oil company in Saudi Arabia, another US ally. Saudi Aramco is one of the largest oil producers in the world. The attack wiped the data from thirty-five thousand Saudi Aramco computers, paralyzing operations and disrupting the flow of oil worldwide. The next month, Iranian cyberattackers hit major US banks with a string of sustained DDoS attacks. Iranian officials said that both of these attacks were retaliation for the US Stuxnet attack.

THE FUTURE WAR TO END ALL WARS

What would happen if the United States went to cyberwar with Russia or Iran? Chances are, the attacks against both sides would be larger, longer, and more numerous than those carried out in previous cyberwars. Attackers would choose targets to create a maximum amount of chaos and destruction. On both sides of the war, targets would probably include these:

Banks and financial institutions. An attack on the computers of major banks might cause all bank balances to drop to zero or keep customers from accessing their funds. An attack on stock market computers might throw world financial markets into turmoil.

Airports and other transportation networks. Previous cyberattacks on rail systems have halted all train traffic in targeted countries. Attacks on airports could disrupt air traffic or even cause planes to crash.

Power plants and utility companies. Imagine a cyberattack that disabled all power systems for days or weeks at a time—no lights, heat, and working traffic signals. This outage would disrupt food supplies as well, since food producers, food distributors, grocery stores, and consumers all rely on electrically powered freezers and refrigerators to keep food from spoiling. Cyberattacks on water facilities, such as systems that control reservoirs and water mains, could block the flow of water to entire cities. An even worse scenario would be a cyberattack on a nuclear power plant. The result could be a meltdown—the melting of the core of a nuclear reactor. Such an event might expose millions of people to deadly radiation.

Hospitals and emergency response teams. An attack on the computer systems of major hospitals could bring medical activity to a halt and result in untold numbers of patient deaths. An attack on police and emergency response systems could make it difficult if not impossible for first responders to deal with crimes, fires, and other emergencies.

Internet, telephone, and communications. Society depends on the internet for information, entertainment, communication, business, and more. Imagine a cyberattack on the internet: no Instagram, Twitter, email, ecommerce, smart lights, or smart door locks, and no way to look up information online. The situation would be worse if cyberattackers disabled telecommunications networks, such as cell phone towers. Not only would business halt, but people couldn't call the police or paramedics. If radio and TV stations were also struck by a cyberattack, no one could get news reports or critical information about how to stay safe.

Government and defense systems. Federal, state, and local governments depend on computer networks and the internet for their services and operations. The military runs its operations and controls many weapons, such as drones and missiles, via computer. If a cyberattack hits military computers, fighting forces couldn't organize a defense, leaving the entire country vulnerable to a physical attack by enemy aircraft, missiles, or troops.

Consider how your life would be disrupted if some or all of these scenarios were to occur. You might wake up one morning to find your home without gas, electricity, water, or a working internet connection. The food in your refrigerator and freezer would begin to spoil.

NATIONAL SECURITY PRESIDENTIAL MEMORANDUM 13

Faced with the likelihood of a future cyberwar, in January 2013 President Barack Obama signed Presidential Policy Directive 20 (PPD 20), which established principles and processes to guide the country's cyberoperations. The document stated that the United States would initiate cyberattacks only after a lengthy process of discussion and approvals by various government agencies. PPD 20 "provides a whole-of-government approach consistent with the values that we promote domestically and internationally." To Obama, it was unthinkable that the United States would initiate a cyberwar, which would most likely have a catastrophic impact on all nations in the conflict, without extremely careful deliberation.

Obama's successor, Donald Trump, felt no such caution. He wanted to strengthen the country's ability to launch a cyberwar. On September 18, 2018, Trump reversed PPD 20 by issuing National Security Presidential Memorandum 13. NSPM 13 gives the US government the authority to use its most powerful cyberweapons offensively.

The president's directive effectively frees the military, without a burdensome bureaucratic approval process, to engage in cyberattacks. John Bolton, the country's national security director when the memorandum was issued, said, with NSPM 13, "our [military's] hands are not tied as they were in the Obama administration."

Many feel that by removing the restrictions of PPD 20, NSPM 13 edges the United States closer to cyberwar. The backers of the new strategy believe it is necessary to counter threatening behavior from US enemies. Bolton defended NSPM 13, saying that it is "in our national interest—not because we want more offensive operations in cyberspace, but precisely to create the structures of deterrence [discouraging enemies from attacking] that will demonstrate to adversaries that the cost of their engaging in operations against us is higher than they want to bear."

Your home heater would have no power, and you would have only clothing and blankets to keep you warm. You couldn't use your cell phone to connect to the internet because cellular networks are down. You might get in a car and find that all the stoplights are blinking red or completely off. Schools and office buildings would be dark, grocery stores closed, and gas pumps inoperable. You couldn't withdraw any cash from the ATM.

You might be able to get by without basic services for a day or two, but what would happen if those days stretch into weeks or months? What would you, your family, and your neighbors do for food and water? Who would protect you if desperate people ran through the streets, looting buildings and homes for food and supplies, and you couldn't contact the police? What if you saw missiles flying overhead, streaking toward nearby targets that the military couldn't defend? Indeed, the consequences of a prolonged cyberwar would be grim—for both civilians and the military, and for those on both sides of the conflict.

PREPARING FOR CYBERWAR

All technologically advanced nations are preparing for cyberwar—both offensively and defensively. Governments know that their countries are dependent on computer systems and networks. They realize how vulnerable they are to attack. Officials know they must enact barriers to potential cyberattacks and even prepare retaliatory attacks on enemy nations.

One frightening aspect of a cyberwar is how quickly it can be launched. A traditional military operation might take months of planning and involve thousands of troops and thousands of pieces of equipment, but a cyberwar can be started with the click of a mouse. One press of a key can activate malware that was injected into an enemy's computer network months or even years earlier. Such long-dormant malware can be fired up and can spread across a network in minutes. That malware can bring down an enemy's power grid, transportation system, or information databases, rendering the country helpless.

CYBERATTACK VULNERABILITY BY NATION

Cyberattack Vulnerability

least

	2–3
	3–4
	4–5
	5–6
	6–7
	7–8
	8–9
	9–10
	10–11
	11–12
	12–13
	13–14
	14–18
	18–20
	20–22

most

NORTH AMERICA

SOUTH AMERICA

To prepare for an attack, some military organizations have installed automated software to retaliate against the enemy as soon as a cyberattack is detected. That eye-for-an-eye approach will result in widespread chaos and destruction for both sides.

Rather than waiting for a cyberwarfare attack, governments can protect against cyberwarfare the same way they protect against other cyberattacks. That includes beefing up cybersecurity measures, installing hardware and software firewalls (software that prevents unauthorized access to a computer), and constantly scanning their systems for malware. But experts say that much of the infrastructure in the United States and other nations is old and outdated, making it vulnerable to cyberattack. Michael S. Rogers, NSA director and former commander of US Cyber Command, warns, "Most of the devices that run the world's infrastructure were never designed to be

EUROPE

ASIA

AFRICA

AUSTRALIA

Source: University of Maryland

This map shows the cyberattack vulnerability of nations around the world. Poor countries, such as most African nations, are the least vulnerable to attack because very few people there have internet connections. The United States, Canada, Australia, and much of Europe have mid-level protection against attacks, since most individuals and businesses use cybersecurity software. The Scandinavian countries have the highest level of cybersecurity. India has the lowest.

secure. The world's critical infrastructure runs on dozens of obscure and old protocols [systems of formatting data]."

Another obstacle to defending against cyberwarfare attacks is the number of potential enemies. In the United States, defense against conventional military attacks tends to focus on those countries with large standing armies, such as China and Russia. But any country with an advanced cyberintelligence organization can carry out effective cyberattacks. The country doesn't need to be big or wealthy or have a big army. A potential cyberwar might be fought against a large country or a small one, such as North Korea or Iran. Cyberattacks are not halted by national boundaries or great distances. Saudi Arabia or India can attack the United States just as readily as can nearby Canada or Mexico. All of this makes preparing for cyberwar challenging.

CHAPTER 9

CYBERSECURITY:
PLAYING DEFENSE

President Barack Obama speaks about cybersecurity at a conference at Stanford University in California in 2015.

The Consumer Electronics Show is one of the biggest conventions in Las Vegas, Nevada. Once a year, thousands of manufacturers and retailers set up exhibits to show off the latest electronics products and technologies. More than 170,000 conference attendees come to Las Vegas to view the exhibits.

In 2020 the Consumer Electronics Show ran from January 7 to 10 and went off without a hitch. But that might not have happened if cyberattackers had had their way. On the opening day of the show, hackers hit the computer systems of the City of Las Vegas. The attack started at 4:30 a.m., when most visitors and city residents were asleep. But the city's IT security office is staffed 24-7, and the early morning staffers noticed unusual activity on the network. Identifying it as a network intrusion (unauthorized access on a computer network), the cybersecurity team immediately tried to protect the system. This included taking the city's website and other internet-based services off-line, before the attackers could do any damage.

Although the perpetrators have not yet been identified or caught, this attack was not unusual. It was just one of 279,000 attempted cyberattacks that hit the City of Las Vegas each month. Besides targeting city computers, cyberattackers also prey on the city's many high-profile casinos. The Las Vegas Sands, the Hard Rock Hotel & Casino, and many other casinos have lost millions of dollars to such attacks.

Security experts believe that the January 2020 attack on the city was likely intended as a ransomware attack. Had the attackers succeeded in locking up the city's data and crippling its computer systems, the damage would have spread to everyone who relied on city services, including conventiongoers attending the electronics show. Conventions, casinos, hotels, and other events and organizations might have been hobbled or shut down completely. But such a catastrophe was averted because of quick-thinking cybersecurity staff. In a series of tweets the day after the attack, city

SOMETHING'S PHISHY

You've probably received phishing emails or text messages. These messages are usually easy to spot. They often contain poor grammar and punctuation, include strange phrasing, and sound as if they weren't written by a native English speaker. In fact, they probably weren't, since a lot of phishing scams originate in eastern European countries.

$$$$$$$$$$$$$$

Joe, your payroll details need updating. Please click below to begin the update.

$$$

UPDATE YOUR ACCOUNT DETAILS

$$$

2/22/2020

Dear Joe Schmoh,

We have detected suspicious activity on your account. As a precaution, we have temporarily deactivated your account and require you to reenter your login credentials using the link above.

Failure to reset your password within 48 hours will result in the permanent deactivation of your account.

Sincerely,

Jaymie Jones

Your account representative

But some phishing emails might fool you because they convincingly appear to come from a company or organization you do business with. If you click on the link in the message, you'll be taken to a website that looks official, complete with the company logo. There, you might be asked to reset your username or password. Don't do it! If you do, you'll likely be exposing yourself to a cyberscam. The criminals are trying to get access to your online accounts, social security number, or other personal information.

To protect yourself from phishing attacks, use common sense. If you suspect that an email or text message is fake, delete it. Don't ever click on the link in a suspicious email or text. A legitimate organization will never send an email or text asking you to click on a link to change your username or password. And if you do need to make such changes, go directly to the organization's website by typing its URL into your browser. Do not click any unrequested link to get there.

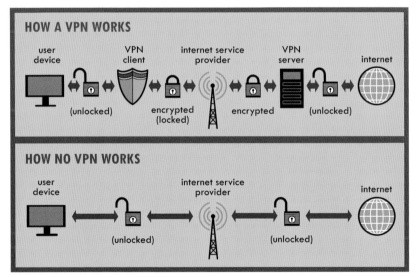

Users can protect themselves from man-in-the-middle attacks and other cyberintrusions by using a virtual private network, or VPN. A VPN encrypts data as it travels across the internet.

CYBERDEFENDERS

The job of cybersecurity staff is to protect computer systems against network intrusion and cyberattacks. The work involves analyzing the host organization's network and data, looking for potential weak spots and threats, and then employing technology to protect vulnerable systems. This technology includes deploying anti-malware tools, installing firewalls, and encrypting data so that only authorized people can access it. Cybersecurity staff are also responsible for responding to intrusions or attacks. This work, called incident response, involves identifying an intrusion in real time, stopping the attack, and then repairing any damage caused by the attack.

Cybersecurity teams must be ready to defend against any type of attack. Sometimes a cyberattack is blatantly obvious, as when ransomware shuts down a network of computers or a DDoS attack drives a website off-line. Other cyberattacks are less noticeable. For instance, a cyberattacker might gain access to a system and install a virus that isn't activated until weeks or months after the initial intrusion. Or an attacker might sneak into a system and steal confidential data. In such attacks, the attacker wants to remain unnoticed to continue long-term operations, returning to the targeted site again and again. And studies show that attackers are very good at hiding their tracks. According to a study by the technology company IBM, it takes an average of 197 days for a company to identify a typical data breach—and another 69 days to shut down the attack. The longer the attack goes undiscovered, the more data the attacker can steal.

How does an organization know when it has been infiltrated? There are often subtle signs, most related to the cyberattack's use of network resources. For example, an IT administrator might notice slowed network traffic because hacker activity is clogging and slowing down the system. Administrators might also notice unusual password activity, such as authorized users being locked out of their accounts and having to reset passwords. Or they might notice large numbers of emails emanating from the network, a sign of an attacker using it to send out mass quantities of phishing or spam messages. Any unusual network activity should be regarded with suspicion.

Once an attack is discovered, it needs to be shut down and the attacker has to be blocked from further access. This may be as simple as barring access from the attacker's IP address (similar to an identification number for a computer or other device). It may require resetting all the network's usernames and passwords. It can even involve shutting down the entire system and rebooting fresh, restoring data from a previous backup, or if the damage is already extensive, rebuilding the system from scratch.

To prepare for attacks, savvy organizations develop an incident response plan. This is a road map or set of instructions for IT staff to follow if their organization is cyberattacked. The plan details what responses should be taken to shut down an attack, how to recover any lost data, and who is responsible for performing specific tasks. This sort of advanced planning helps companies and other organizations more quickly recover from cyberattacks. When an attack happens, the IT staff pulls out the incident response plan and follows the prepared instructions.

PROTECTING AGAINST CYBERATTACKS

Organizations should not wait until they're attacked to beef up cybersecurity. Businesses, government agencies, and other potential targets need to put into place technological and other defenses for all likely types of cyberattacks. They also need to keep those defenses up to date as cybersecurity specialists discover new types of malware and attacks.

One of the most important things any organization can do to guard against cyberattacks is to conduct a cybersecurity risk assessment. This involves a data audit (identifying at-risk data and equipment), a security assessment (evaluating the current state of the organization's data security), and a threat assessment (identifying potential threats against the organization's data and systems). Once the vulnerabilities and threats are identified, the organization can develop specific strategies for protecting its computers.

The United Kingdom's National Cyber Security Centre recommends that organizations follow these steps to reduce the risk of cyberattack:

If an employee falls for a phishing email, they can unknowingly expose their company to a cyberattack.

- Employ firewalls and other software to block access from untrustworthy websites and to keep users from downloading files likely to contain malware.
- Install anti-malware software to detect and delete known malware.
- Regularly and immediately patch known bugs (flaws) and vulnerabilities in computer software and operating systems that hackers could exploit to gain unauthorized access.
- Whitelist (approve access to) known safe websites and blacklist (block access to) known dangerous ones.
- Use software designed to prevent malware from automatically running or installing itself on network devices.
- Make sure that all devices connected to the network, including personal devices such as mobile phones, have protection against malware.
- Enact a policy that requires long, complicated, not easily guessed, and frequently changed passwords.
- Employ access control to limit what apps and devices users can use on the network. (For example, an organization might restrict employees from using USB drives brought from home.)
- Actively monitor unexpected or suspicious network activity.
- Strongly encrypt all valuable data and employee communications.

HOW TO PROTECT YOURSELF FROM CYBERTHREATS

What can you do to protect your personal computer, mobile phone, or tablet from cyberattacks? First, install anti-malware software on your device. This software will detect and stop most known computer viruses, spyware, and other malicious software.

Most computers come with firewall software. Check your computer settings to make sure that this software is enabled. On your home network, make sure your Wi-Fi network is protected by a long and complex password.

Be on the alert for phishing messages and other social engineering attacks. Don't click links in emails and text messages, even if the messages appear to be from someone you know or a company you do business with.

If a website requires you to create a password, make sure it's a long and complicated one, with a mix of uppercase and lowercase letters, numbers, and special characters. Do not use the same password for more than one different site, and never use an easily guessed password, such as your dog's name.

Finally, avoid putting too much personal information online. The more personal the information you put online, the easier it is for cyberattackers to guess your passwords or to construct spear phishing campaigns tailored specifically to fool you. If

Phones are just as vulnerable to hacking as any other device. Protect all your devices with anti-malware software.

you suspect that an online communication might be malicious, delete it. If you are being harassed or threatened online, tell a parent, a teacher, or law enforcement.

All these efforts are tools of cybersecurity. To protect against potential cyberattacks, all companies, educational organizations, and government agencies need to use them. They also need to have trained cybersecurity staff ready to respond to attacks.

PEOPLE ARE AS IMPORTANT AS TECHNOLOGY

The final and perhaps most important thing an organization can do to defend against cyberattack is to train its employees properly. All the people in the organization need to know that their own individual efforts are part of cybersecurity.

In particular, employees need to be trained to recognize and block phishing emails and other forms of social engineering. A startlingly large number of intrusions occur because a single employee clicked on a link in a phishing email and unwittingly provided their login credentials. Falling for a phishing scheme is like leaving your key in the door lock. It makes it easy for an intruder to access not just a single account but an entire computer system. The bottom line is that all the cybersecurity technologies in the world don't matter if employees do careless things.

KEEPING UP WITH THE BAD GUYS

Given the numerous and varied threats to computer networks, keeping them secure is a constantly evolving challenge. Cybersecurity experts and cyberattackers are engaged in an ongoing game of cat and mouse, with the good guys continually devising new security methods, the bad guys continually using new techniques to try to breach these defenses, and on and on in an endless cycle.

To stay one step ahead of the cybercriminals, cyberextortionists, and cyberterrorists trying to break into their systems, cybersecurity staff must continually update their anti-malware software. When an attacker does manage to breach a system, cybersecurity experts can often identify the criminal by analyzing the method and malware used—since certain groups tend to use the same techniques and viruses more than once. The damage to the computer network might already be done, but knowing which group perpetrated the attack can lead to an arrest or might at least enable cybersecurity teams to do better in guarding against that attacker in the future.

The reality is that the world of cybersecurity is constantly changing. New threats appear virtually every day and must be secured against. If the cybersecurity experts don't keep up, the bad guys will get ahead of them—and get into their systems.

COVID-19 HACK

In July 2020, governments in Canada, the United Kingdom, and the United States revealed that the Russian hacking group Cozy Bear had tried to steal research related to developing a vaccine for COVID-19. Cozy Bear tried to infiltrate the computers of various universities, medical companies, and health-care organizations, including Britain's Oxford University and the pharmaceutical company AstraZeneca.

The apparent goal of this cyberespionage was to steal information that would help Russia more quickly develop its own COVID-19 vaccine. The hacking attempts involved phishing emails and malware designed to trick employees into revealing their login credentials and passwords. Britain's National Cyber Security Centre says there is no evidence that any data was stolen, although several Oxford scientists noted similarities between their research and work reported by Russian scientists. So it's possible that Cozy Bear did steal some data and pass it along to Russian vaccine researchers.

CHAPTER 10

WANT TO BE A CYBERSPY?

Computer engineering students learn to defend against cyberattacks at a university in France.

Cybersecurity is a growing field. Big and small businesses, government agencies, educational institutions, and other organizations are all beefing up their IT and cybersecurity to defend against a growing number of cyberthreats. Many national

PREPARING FOR A CAREER AS A CYBERSPY

Whether you'd like to work in cyberintelligence or cybersecurity for the government, join a private consulting firm, or run your own cybersecurity business, you need a certain set of skills. Cyberintelligence and cybersecurity specialists need to know a lot about computers, networks, and application programming.

To land a high-paying cyberjob, study computer science, information technology, or a related technical field. Colleges, trade schools, and technical schools offer this training. Some cybersecurity experts even train themselves without school, using a wide variety of tech-focused books, videos, and online training courses.

The best strategy is to obtain a four-year bachelor's degree in a technical field from an accredited college or university. Most schools will require you to take basic classes in computer programming and network design and will also let you take elective courses in more specialized areas. For example, if you're getting a computer science degree from the University of California, you can take elective undergraduate courses in internet and network security, cyberwar, and cryptography, among other topics.

For more senior positions in the cyberworkforce, a graduate degree may be required. Many universities offer advanced degrees in specialized areas of cybertechnology. For example, Indiana University offers a master's of science degree in cybersecurity risk management. The University of Minnesota offers a master's degree in security technology.

Besides getting a university education, many cyberprofessionals

```
# 3) if server_capabilities
wp = EOFPacketWrapper(packet)
self.warning_count = wp.warning_count
self.has_next = wp.has_next
return True

def _read_result_packet(self, first_packet):
    self.field_count = first_packet.read_length
    self._get_descriptions()
    self._read_rowdata_packet()
```

Those who want a career in cybersecurity must know how to read and create computer code.

enhance their skill sets and résumés by obtaining professional certification in specialized technical areas. For instance, you could train to become a certified ethical (noncriminal) hacker, a certified information security manager, or a certified information systems security professional. Such certifications will make you more attractive to future employers.

EVALUATING POTENTIAL CYBERJOBS

Businesses, government agencies, and other organizations employ many different kinds of cyberintelligence and cybersecurity experts. Most share a similar skill set, although each is tasked with specific responsibilities. Here are some of the more common cyberjobs:

- Capability development specialists update an organization's systems to protect them against new cyberthreats.
- Chief information security officers are in charge of the entire cybersecurity of a large company, reporting directly to the company's chief executive officer or president.
- Cryptoanalysts, sometimes called cryptographers, decipher encrypted messages and look for signs of infiltration, as well

as develop ciphers and encrypt their own organization's data.
- Cyberintelligence analysts do technical research and analysis of cyberthreats and create threat intelligence reports for decision makers such as government officials.
- Cybersecurity analysts detect and prevent cyberattacks via various technological methods.
- Cybersecurity researchers design and recommend new cybersecurity technologies and techniques.
- Cyberthreat analysts identify global cyberthreats.
- Exploitation analysts, also called ethical hackers, or penetration testers, hack into systems to identify vulnerabilities that could be exploited by malicious hackers.
- Forensics experts detect and analyze digital footprints left behind by intrusions or suspicious activity.
- Incident responders address and reduce the effects of ongoing cyberattacks and other threats.
- Information security engineers provide systems engineering and support communications systems.
- Operators in the military gain, maintain, and control computing platforms on active missions.
- Vulnerability analysts analyze networks and systems for signs of possible cyberattacks and recommend ways to improve vulnerabilities.

With cybercrime and cyberattacks at all-time record levels, the demand for cybersecurity professionals of all types is strong. According to the US Bureau of Labor Statistics, the number of cybersecurity jobs is expected to increase by 32 percent between 2018 and 2028.

This high demand also helps keep salaries high as different entities compete for a limited number of skilled workers. The bureau reports that in May 2018, the average annual wage for a cybersecurity analyst was $98,350. The top earners made more than $156,580 a year.

ETHICAL HACKING

When most people think of hackers, they think of cybercriminals, cyberterrorists, and other lawbreakers intent on stealing data and damaging computer systems. In cybersecurity these criminals are called black hat hackers.

But not all hackers are bad guys. Some hackers do their work for good rather than evil purposes. These white hat or ethical hackers break into computer systems with the goal of discovering their vulnerabilities. Then the host organization can patch (repair) those vulnerabilities to create a more secure system. Companies, governments, and other organizations often employ white hat hackers to make their computer systems stronger.

WHERE TO FIND A CYBERSECURITY JOB

Organizations of all types and sizes want to build their cybersecurity staffs. Large companies with big IT departments often have separate cybersecurity staffers, typically led by a chief information security officer. Small companies typically incorporate cybersecurity into their general IT department. The companies aren't big enough to maintain separate cybersecurity staff, so one or more IT employees does double duty with cybersecurity activities. Some small companies don't even have IT departments. Instead, they hire outside firms to handle IT and cybersecurity.

Schools, school districts, and other nonprofit organizations often have strong IT departments with dedicated cybersecurity staff. Government agencies at all levels—national, state, and local— typically have large IT and cybersecurity staffs. So the public sector is a good source for cybersecurity jobs, especially as cities, states, and the federal government prepare against and respond to an increasing wave of ransomware and other cyberattacks.

Symantec and other cybersecurity firms specialize in keeping computer systems safe from attack.

The military is also a good source of cybersecurity jobs. The United States continues to beef up its defensive and offensive cyberwarfare capabilities, which means lots of open positions for qualified cyberprofessionals.

Many cybersecurity professionals work for independent contractors and consulting firms. These workers get their paycheck from the consulting firm but work day-to-day with client businesses, including sometimes government agencies. Often that means working at the client's offices, either short term or long term.

THE FUTURE OF CYBERSECURITY

As our world has become increasingly connected thanks to the growth of the internet and advancement of technology, cyberthreats have grown. The technology that makes our world better also opens up new opportunities for abuse and exploitation. The internet is a wonderful tool that enriches our lives, but bad guys use this tool to steal and wreak havoc too.

In the United States, most people have multiple online accounts: for retail purchases, email, credit cards and banking, music and movie streaming services, social media, newspaper subscriptions, libraries, ride-hailing services, phone service, Wi-Fi, and much more. No matter where you live, how you make a living, or where you go to school, you can't ignore the internet. So no one can ignore cyberthreats and cybersecurity. The risk of cyberattack of all kinds is constantly growing. The more devices we connect to the internet and the more data we store there, the more material there is for hackers and other malicious actors to steal, harm, or destroy. Cyberattacks are likely to become more common and more damaging for organizations and individuals.

With every new threat, however, comes a new opportunity to protect against that threat. Governments, corporations, and other institutions are all beefing up their cybersecurity staff to guard against an increasing number of cyberthreats. So it's a good time to be in the cybersecurity business.

It's also a good time to be a cyberspy, whether for the government or some other entity. As the old saying goes, the best defense is a strong offense, and countries around the world appear to agree. Whether or not a full-scale cyberwar erupts in your lifetime, the use of targeted cyberattacks against global enemies is likely to increase. So if your talent is technical and you like either security or spying, then a cybersecurity career may be just right for you.

GLOSSARY

BACKDOOR: a way to bypass normal security measures to access a computer system. Once a backdoor is established, an attacker can use it again and again.

BITCOIN: digital currency used for online transactions. Unlike traditional currency, Bitcoin does not exist in the form of bills or coins. It is not issued or controlled by a central bank.

BOT: short for *robot*, a software application that automatically performs tasks online. Some bots run fake social media accounts. Other bots are used in DDoS and other cyberattacks.

BOTNET: a network of bots or "zombie" computers and devices remotely controlled by an attacker

CLASSIFIED: kept secret by the government for reasons of national security

CONFIRMATION BIAS: the tendency to believe information that confirms one's existing beliefs

CRYPTOCURRENCY: a digital, encrypted currency such as Bitcoin

CRYPTOGRAPHY: the practice of writing and breaking secret codes

CYBERBULLYING: threatening or bullying a person via social media or other internet-based communications

CYBERESPIONAGE: using the internet and computer networks to illegally access private data

CYBEREXTORTION: using ransomware to freeze data, a computer network, or a website until a ransom is paid

CYBERSECURITY: protecting websites and computer networks from malware and cyberattacks

CYBERSTALKING: using social media and other internet-based communications to follow or harass someone

CYBERTERRORISM: politically motivated crimes and attacks on computer systems, designed to disrupt business, communications, and government networks; sow fear; and endanger lives and property

DECRYPTION: deciphering coded messages

DISINFORMATION: false information spread deliberately to influence public opinion or to obscure the truth

DISTRIBUTED DENIAL OF SERVICE (DDOS) ATTACK: an attack in which a group of computers sends a massive number of messages to overwhelm and disable a website or network

ECHO CHAMBER: an online environment in which people encounter only opinions and beliefs similar to their own. Social media enables echo chambers by linking people who share one another's views.

ENCRYPTION: encoding data into a form that can be accessed by only certain users. Cybersecurity staff often use encryption to protect data from cyberattacks. During ransomware attacks, cyberattackers might use encryption to prevent authorized users from accessing their own data.

ETHICAL HACKER: a person who hacks into a computer network to test or evaluate its security. If ethical hackers find a vulnerability, they can tell the network administrator how to fix it.

FAKE NEWS: news items or social media posts that are designed to look like real news stories but are mostly or wholly untrue

FIREWALL: a software barrier designed to block unauthorized access to a computer network

HACKER: a person who gains unauthorized access to a computer or network

HACKTIVIST: someone who hacks into computers to advance a political agenda. Hacktivists might disable the websites of organizations they oppose or take over the sites to send their own messages.

HONEYPOT: a website or server designed to attract cyberattackers. A honeypot might contain fake or useless data. Once the honeypot is attacked, cyberdefenders can figure out who the attacker is and how to keep the attacker from getting valuable data.

IMPLICIT BIAS: an automatic and unconscious prejudice against or opinion about a member of a certain racial, ethnic, religious, or other group

INFORMATION TECHNOLOGY (IT): the use of computer systems for data storage and communications

INTELLECTUAL PROPERTY: work that is the result of human intelligence, such as a manuscript, a design, or an invention

MALWARE: short for *malicious software*, any software (such as computer viruses, worms, and spyware) designed to disrupt, damage, or allow unauthorized access to data or computer systems

MAN-IN-THE-MIDDLE (MITM) ATTACK: a cyberattack in which the intruder intercepts messages between a user and a computer network or website. The intruder can then steal login credentials and other private information or pose as the user to plant malware.

MISINFORMATION: false or misleading information, often deliberately intended to deceive

PHISHING: using fake email messages and fake websites to trick people into revealing usernames and passwords

PROPAGANDA: biased or misleading information, often used to promote a particular political cause

RANSOMWARE: a type of malware that freezes a victim's data, computer network, or website until money is paid

SOCIAL ENGINEERING: manipulating human behavior, often by trickery. Phishing attacks, which trick computer users into revealing usernames and passwords, are examples of social engineering.

SPEAR PHISHING: a phishing attack with a fake message personalized to fool a specific victim

SQL INJECTION ATTACK: a cyberattack that injects malicious code into a database running the SQL programming language

VIRUS: malware that remains dormant on a computer until an infected program or file is activated. After that, the virus reproduces itself and infects the computer.

WORM: malware that automatically reproduces itself once it enters a computer. Unlike a virus, a worm doesn't have to wait for an infected file or program to be activated.

ZOMBIE: a hijacked computer used in a cyberattack

SOURCE NOTES

5   Jura Koncius, "Targeting Tweens: Retailers Are Homing in on the Next Generation," *Washington Post*, March 23, 2000, https://www.washingtonpost .com/wp-srv/WPcap/2000-03/23/088r-032300-idx.html.

6   Loren Sands-Ramshaw, "The NSA: An Inside View," *Loren's Blog*, December 10, 2013, http://lorensr.me/nsa-an-inside-view.html.

6   Sands-Ramshaw.

7   Sands-Ramshaw.

7   Sands-Ramshaw.

8   Sands-Ramshaw.

9   "Army Cyber Command Employee Reviews," Indeed, accessed November 12, 2019, https://www.indeed.com/cmp/Army-Cyber-Command/reviews.

9   "Army Cyber Command."

9   Ellen Nakashima and Aaron Gregg, "NSA's Top Talent Is Leaving Because of Low Pay, Slumping Morale and Unpopular Reorganization," *Washington Post,* January 2, 2018, https://www.washingtonpost.com/world/national -security/the-nsas-top-talent-is-leaving-because-of-low-pay-and-battered -morale/2018/01/02/ff19f0c6-ec04-11e7-9f92-10a2203f6c8d_story.html.

9   Charles S. Clark, "NSA Director: The Agency 'Sells Itself' to Potential Recruits," *Government Executive*, August 10, 2018, https://www.govexec .com/defense/2018/08/nsa-director-agency-sells-itself-potential-recruits /150451/.

12   Dina Temple-Raston, "How the U.S. Hacked ISIS," NPR, September 26, 2019, https://www.npr.org/2019/09/26/763545811/how-the-u-s-hacked-isis.

22   Laken Howard, "Is It a Good Idea to Research Someone Online before a First Date? Here's What Experts Say," *Bustle*, January 8, 2019, https:// www.bustle.com/p/is-it-a-good-idea-to-research-someone-online-before-a -first-date-heres-what-experts-say-15580568.

23   Darcel Rockett, "How Much Pre-Date Cyber Stalking Is Healthy? Chicago Dating Expert Weighs In," *Chicago Tribune*, January 11, 2019, https:// www.chicagotribune.com/lifestyles/ct-life-online-dating-research-20190109 -story.html.

25–26   Anthony Cuthbertson, "Iranian Hackers Attack UK Universities to Steal Secret Research," *Independent* (London), August 24, 2018, https:// www.independent.co.uk/life-style/gadgets-and-tech/news/iran-hackers -uk-university-cyber-attack-security-cobalt-dickens-a8506406.html.

26   "Espionage," Merriam-Webster.com, accessed December 10, 2019, https:// www.merriam-webster.com/dictionary/espionage.

28   David Brunnstrom and Jim Finkle, "U.S. Considers 'Proportional' Response to Sony Hacking Attack," Reuters, December 18, 2014, https://www.reuters .com/article/us-sony-cybersecurity-northkorea/u-s-considers-proportional -response-to-sony-hacking-attack-idUSKBN0JW24Z20141218.

35 Hilary Krieger, "An Introduction to the Dark Arts of Opposition Research," FiveThirtyEight, October 31, 2017, https://fivethirtyeight.com/features/an-introduction-to-the-dark-arts-of-opposition-research/.

36 Andy Kroll, "There Have Been 800-Plus Political Cyberattacks in the Past Year Alone," *Rolling Stone*, September 30, 2019, https://www.rollingstone.com/politics/politics-news/cyberattack-election-meddling-democracy-2020-892623/.

41 Michael Grothaus, "Russian Trolls Were Reportedly Ordered to Watch 'House of Cards,'" *Fast Company*, October 16, 2017, https://www.fastcompany.com/40481465/russian-trolls-were-reportedly-ordered-to-watch-house-of-cards-to-turn-americans-against-their-own-government.

41 Grothaus.

42 Jack Crowe, "Senate Intel Committee Confirms Russians Hacked Election Systems in 50 States, Didn't Change Vote Totals," *National Review*, July 26, 2019, https://www.nationalreview.com/news/senate-intel-committee-confirms-russians-hacked-election-systems-in-50-states-didnt-change-vote-totals/.

42 Ari Berman, "American Democracy Is Now Under Siege by Both Cyber-Espionage and GOP Voter Suppression," *Nation*, July 12, 2017, https://www.thenation.com/article/american-democracy-is-now-under-siege-by-both-cyber-espionage-and-gop-voter-suppression/.

42 Jen Schwartz, "The Vulnerabilities of Our Voting Machines," *Scientific American*, November 1, 2018, https://www.scientificamerican.com/article/the-vulnerabilities-of-our-voting-machines/.

46 Michael Isikoff, "Exclusive: The True Origins of the Seth Rich Conspiracy Theory," Yahoo! News, July 9, 2019, https://news.yahoo.com/exclusive-the-true-origins-of-the-seth-rich-conspiracy-a-yahoo-news-investigation-100000831.html.

46 Isikoff.

47 Isikoff.

49 Tamara Keith, "President Trump's Description of What's 'Fake' Is Expanding," NPR, September 2, 2018, https://www.npr.org/2018/09/02/643761979/president-trumps-description-of-whats-fake-is-expanding.

50 Craig Timberg and Tony Romm, "It's Not Just the Russians Anymore as Iranians and Others Turn Up Disinformation Efforts Ahead of the 2020 Vote," *Washington Post*, July 25, 2019, https://www.washingtonpost.com/technology/2019/07/25/its-not-just-russians-anymore-iranians-others-turn-up-disinformation-efforts-ahead-vote/.

51 Alicia Hernan (@AliciaHernan3), "That stupid moron doesn't get that that by creating bad guys, spewing hate filled words and creating fear of 'others', his message is spreading to fanatics around the world. Or maybe he does," Twitter, March 16, 2019 (account deleted).

54 Brian Resnick, "The Science behind Why Fake News Is So Hard to Wipe Out," Vox, October 31, 2017, https://www.vox.com/science-and-health/2017/10/5/16410912/illusory-truth-fake-news-las-vegas-google-facebook.

55 Sabrina Siddiqui, "Half of All Americans See Fake News as Bigger Threat Than Terrorism, Study Finds," *Guardian* (US edition), June 7, 2019, https://www.theguardian.com/us-news/2019/jun/06/fake-news-how-misinformation-became-the-new-front-in-us-political-warfare.

57 Chris Sienko, "Ransomware Case Studies: Hollywood Presbyterian and the Ottawa Hospital," Infosec, accessed December 28, 2019, https://resources.infosecinstitute.com/category/healthcare-information-security/healthcare-attack-statistics-and-case-studies/ransomware-case-studies-hollywood-presbyterian-and-the-ottawa-hospital/.

58 Danny Yadron, "Los Angeles Hospital Paid $17,000 in Bitcoin to Ransomware Attackers," *Guardian* (US edition), February 17, 2016, https://www.theguardian.com/technology/2016/feb/17/los-angeles-hospital-hacked-ransom-bitcoin-hollywood-presbyterian-medical-center.

61 Allen Kim, "In the Last 10 Months, 140 Local Governments, Police Stations and Hospitals Have Been Held Hostage by Ransomware Attacks," CNN, October 8, 2019, https://www.cnn.com/2019/10/08/business/ransomware-attacks-trnd/index.html.

64 "The State of Ransomware in the US: Report and Statistics 2019," Emsisoft Malware Lab, December 12, 2019, https://blog.emsisoft.com/en/34822/the-state-of-ransomware-in-the-us-report-and-statistics-2019/.

64 John Simerman, "Ransomware in New Orleans Attack Is Likely Organized Crime," *Government Technology*, December 18, 2019, https://www.govtech.com/security/Ransomware-in-New-Orleans-Attack-Is-Likely-Organized-Crime.html.

72 "A Letter from Concerned Scientists," *Frontline,* February 27, 2002, https://www.pbs.org/wgbh/pages/frontline/shows/cyberwar/etc/letter.html.

72 Thomas Oriti, "Cyberterrorists Targeting Healthcare Systems, Critical Infrastructure," Australian Broadcasting System, October 23, 2017, https://www.abc.net.au/news/2017-10-23/forget-explosives,-terrorists-are-coming-after-cyber-systems/9076786.

72 Oriti.

74 Yohah Jeremy Bob, "EXCLUSIVE: Israel Needs to Be Ready for Terrorist 'Dirty' Cyber Bomb," *Jerusalem Post*, September 12, 2019, https://www.jpost.com/Israel-News/EXCLUSIVE-Israel-needs-to-be-ready-for-terrorist-dirty-cyber-bomb-601523.

74 Daniel R. Coats, *Worldwide Threat Assessment of the US Intelligence Community*, Senate Select Committee on Intelligence, January 29, 2019, https://www.dni.gov/files/ODNI/documents/2019-ATA-SFR---SSCI.pdf.

76 Richard Clarke, "What Are Al Quada's Capabilities?," *Frontline*, April 14, 2003, https://www.pbs.org/wgbh/pages/frontline/shows/cyberwar/vulnerable/alqaeda.html.

76 "Department of Homeland Security's (DHS's) Role in Critical Infrastructure Protection (CIP) Cybersecurity," Government Accountability Office, May 2005, https://www.us-cert.gov/ics/content/cyber-threat-source-descriptions.

77 Helene Cooper, "ISIS Is Cited in Hacking of Central Command's Twitter and YouTube Accounts," *New York Times*, January 12, 2015, https://www.nytimes.com/2015/01/13/us/isis-is-cited-in-hacking-of-central-commands-twitter-feed.html.

77 Stephen McBride, "IAN BREMMER: Cyberterrorism Is Coming—and That Worries Me a Lot," Business Insider, June 7, 2017, https://www.businessinsider.com/bremmer-on-future-of-cyberterrorism-2017-6.

80 David Gilbert, "Inside the Massive Cyber War between Russia and Ukraine," *Vice*, March 29, 2019, https://www.vice.com/en_us/article/bjqe8m/inside-the-massive-cyber-war-between-russia-and-ukraine.

86 "Presidential Policy Directive 20," Homeland Security Digital Library, January 2013, https://www.hsdl.org/?abstract&did=814897.

86 Ellen Nakashima, "White House Authorizes 'Offensive Cyber Operations' to Deter Foreign Adversaries," *Washington Post*, September 20, 2018, https://www.washingtonpost.com/world/national-security/trump-authorizes-offensive-cyber-operations-to-deter-foreign-adversaries-bolton-says/2018/09/20/b5880578-bd0b-11e8-b7d2-0773aa1e33da_story.html.

86 Nakashima.

88–89 Chloe Albanesius, "Cyberwar Is Here: Are You Ready?," *PC Magazine*, September 19, 2019, https://www.pcmag.com/news/370753/cyberwar-is-here-are-you-ready.

91 Catalin Cimpanu, quoting the City of Las Vegas Twitter feed, "City of Las Vegas Said It Successfully Avoided Devastating Cyber-Attack," ZDNet, January 9, 2020, https://www.zdnet.com/article/city-of-las-vegas-said-it-successfully-avoided-devastating-cyber-attack/.

SELECTED BIBLIOGRAPHY

Clarke, Richard A., and Robert Knake. *Cyber War: The Next Threat to National Security and What to Do about It*. New York: Ecco, 2011.

De Groot, Juliana. "A History of Ransomware Attacks: The Biggest and Worst Ransomware Attacks of All Time." Digital Guardian. Accessed January 7, 2020. https://www.digitalguardian.com/blog/history-ransomware-attacks-biggest-and-worst-ransomware-attacks-all-time.

Dishman, Lydia. "How I Got My Dream Job as a Cybersleuth." *Fast Company*, March 31, 2017. https://www.fastcompany.com/3069270/how-i-got-my-dream-job-as-a-cybersleuth.

Greenberg, Andy. "The WIRED Guide to Cyberwar." *Wired*, August 23, 2019. https://www.wired.com/story/cyberwar-guide.

Kirtley, Jane E. "Getting to the Truth: Fake News, Libel Laws, and 'Enemies of the American People.'" American Bar Association. Accessed December 24, 2019. https://www.americanbar.org/groups/crsj/publications/human_rights_magazine_home/the-ongoing-challenge-to-define-free-speech/getting-to-the-truth/.

Palmer, Danny. "30 Years of Ransomware: How One Bizarre Attack Laid the Foundations for the Malware Taking Over the World." ZDNet, December 19, 2019. https://www.zdnet.com/article/30-years-of-ransomware-how-one-bizarre-attack-laid-the-foundations-for-the-malware-taking-over-the-world/.

"Public Service Announcement: High Impact Ransomware Attacks Threaten US Businesses and Organizations." Federal Bureau of Investigation. Accessed December 20, 2019. https://www.ic3.gov/media/2019/191002.aspx.

Ranger, Steve. "What Is Cyberwar? Everything You Need to Know about the Frightening Future of Digital Conflict." ZDNet, December 4, 2019. https://www.zdnet.com/article/cyberwar-a-guide-to-the-frightening-future-of-online-conflict/.

Tesauro, Lyda. "The Role Al Qaeda Plays in Cyberterrorism." Small Wars Journal. Accessed December 30, 2019. https://smallwarsjournal.com/jrnl/art/role-al-qaeda-plays-cyberterrorism.

Wheeler, Tarah. "In Cyberwar, There Are No Rules." *Foreign Policy*, September 12, 2018. https://foreignpolicy.com/2018/09/12/in-cyberwar-there-are-no-rules-cybersecurity-war-defense/.

FURTHER INFORMATION

BOOKS

Gitlin, Martin, and Margaret J. Goldstein. *Cyber Attack*. Minneapolis: Twenty-First Century Books, 2015.

Greenberg, Andy. *Sandworm: A New Era of Cyberwar and the Hunt for the Kremlin's Most Dangerous Hackers*. New York: Doubleday, 2019.

January, Brendon. *Information Security: Privacy under Siege*. Minneapolis: Twenty-First Century Books, 2016.

Miller, Michael. *Fake News: Separating Truth from Fiction*. Minneapolis: Twenty-First Century Books, 2019.

Sciutto, Jim. *The Shadow War: Inside Russia's and China's Secret Operations to Defeat America*. New York: Harper, 2019.

Timmons, Angie, and Sara L. Latta. *Investigating Cybercrime*. New York: Enslow, 2018.

Wiener, Gary. *Cyberterrorism and Ransomware Attacks*. New York: Greenhaven, 2018.

FILMS AND VIDEOS

Cyberwar. New York: Vice Media, 2016–2017.
This fascinating two-season documentary television series covers the entire gamut of cybersecurity, cyberterrorism, and cyberwar. Host Ben Makuch travels around the world, talking with hackers, government officials, and other surveillance professionals.

Cyber War. Surrey, UK: Journeyman Pictures, 2016.
This short documentary examines the threat of online attacks, cyberespionage, and nation-to-nation cyberwar.

The Defenders. Boston: Cybereason, 2018.
This documentary offers a behind-the-scenes look at four famous cyberattacks, focusing on the cybersecurity professionals tasked with defending against them.

Zero Days. New York: Magnolia Pictures, 2016.
This critically acclaimed documentary focuses on the Stuxnet computer virus and the US cyberoperation to disable Iran's nuclear weapons program.

WEBSITES

Careers in Cybersecurity
https://www.careersincybersecurity.com
This site is a gateway for a variety of information about cybersecurity careers, education, and resources. It includes a cybersecurity blog and career guide.

"Cybercrime and Cyberwar: A Spotter's Guide to the Groups That Are Out to Get You"
https://www.zdnet.com/article/cybercrime-and-cyberwar-a-spotters-guide-to
-the-groups-that-are-out-to-get-you/
This is a comprehensive guide to malicious hackers, hacktivist groups, criminal gangs, terrorist groups, and more that are operating in cyberspace.

"Cyber Security Degrees and Careers: How to Work in Cyber Security"
https://www.learnhowtobecome.org/computer-careers/cyber-security/
This page details the steps to start a career in cybersecurity, including recommended skills, college courses and degrees, certificates, and additional training.

Cyber Warfare
https://www.rand.org/topics/cyber-warfare.html
Compiled by the Rand Corporation, this is a continually updated collection of reports, news articles, blog posts, and commentary regarding the threat of cyberwar.

Free Ethical Hacking Tutorials
https://www.guru99.com/ethical-hacking-tutorials.html
Here you'll find a large selection of free tutorials teaching the various tools and techniques used by ethical (and nonethical) hackers, including social engineering, password cracking, DDoS attacks, SQL injection, and cryptography.

Hacker News
https://www.thehackernews.com
This popular blog from tech expert Paul Graham provides daily cybersecurity and technology news and opinion. It is one of the most recognized sources of information for the cybersecurity industry.

"Students, Launch Your Cybersecurity Careers"
https://niccs.us-cert.gov/formal-education/students-launch-your-cyber-career
From the government's National Initiative of Cybersecurity Careers and Studies, this is a detailed and interactive guide to various cybersecurity careers and the education.

"What Is Cyber Security? What You Need to Know"
https://us.norton.com/internetsecurity-malware-what-is-cybersecurity-what
-you-need-to-know.html
The Norton cybersecurity firm offers a general overview of cybersecurity, cyberthreats, and how to protect against cyberattacks.

INDEX

ABOUT THE AUTHOR

Michael Miller is a prolific and best-selling author. He has written more than two hundred nonfiction books on a variety of topics, including *Fake News: Separating Fact from Fiction* and *Exposing Hate: Prejudice, Hatred, and Violence in Action*, both published in 2019. Miller lives with his wife, several stepchildren, and seven grandchildren in the Twin Cities area of Minnesota.

PHOTO ACKNOWLEDGMENTS

Image credits: National Security Agency, p. 4; PictureLux/The Hollywood Archive/ Alamy Stock Photo, p. 6; © U.S. Air Force photo by William Belcher, p. 8; Laura Westlund/Independent Picture Service, pp. 11, 22, 23, 39, 53, 60, 67, 88–89, 92, 93; Chip Somodevilla/Getty Images, p. 12; National Archives, p. 14; Melina Mara-Pool/Getty Images, p. 21; Jerry Cleveland/The Denver Post/Getty Images, p. 24; OBYN BECK/AFP/Getty Images, p. 28; CHEN PENG/flickr, p. 31; Capt. Hans Zeiger/United States Department of Defense, p. 34; Hulton Archive/Getty Images, p. 36; Bill Clark/CQ Roll Cal/Getty Images, p. 41; Paul Hennessy/Alamy Live News/Alamy Stock Photo, p. 44; Jason Kempin/Getty Images for Politicon, p. 47; MikhailBerkut /Shutterstock.com, p. 51; Junkyardsparkle/Wikimedia Commons (Public Domain), p. 56; ROB ENGELAAR/AFP/Getty Images, p. 63; Trong Nguyen/ Shutterstock.com, p. 70; Jaap Arriens/NurPhoto/Getty Images, p. 75; DC Studio/ Shutterstock.com, p. 76; jeffadl/iStockphoto/Getty Images, p. 78; DIMITAR DILKOFF/AFP/Getty Images, p. 82; IIPA/Getty Images, p. 83; NICHOLAS KAMM/ AFP/Getty Images, p. 90; Flamingo Images/Shutterstock.com, p. 96; Antonio Guillem/Shutterstock.com, p. 97; FRED TANNEAU/AFP/Getty Images, p. 100; Pentao10/Shutterstock.com, p. 102;

Cover: MR.Cole_Photographer/Moment/Getty Images; Djent/Shutterstock.com.